M000318205

Who Look at Me?!

Personal/Public Scholarship

VOLUME 3

Series Editor

Patricia Leavy (*USA*)

Editorial Board

Carolyn Ellis (*University of South Florida, USA*)
Donna Y. Ford (*Vanderbilt University, USA*)
Henry Giroux (*McMaster University, Canada*)
Stacy Holman Jones (*Monash University, Australia*)
Sut Jhally (*University of Massachusetts, USA*)
Kip Jones (*Bournemouth University, UK*)
Jean Kilbourne, (*Wellesley Centers for Women, USA*)
Peter McLaren (*Chapman University, USA*)

Scope

The *Personal/Public Scholarship* book series values: (1) public scholarship (scholarship that is accessible to academic and popular audiences), and (2) interconnections between the personal and public in all areas of cultural, social, economic and political life. We publish textbooks, monographs and anthologies (original material only).

Please consult www.patricialeavy.com for submission requirements (click the book series tab).

The titles published in this series are listed at *brill.com/pepu*

Who Look at Me?!

*Shifting the Gaze of Education through
Blackness, Queerness, and the Body*

By

Durell M. Callier and Dominique C. Hill

BRILL

SENSE

LEIDEN | BOSTON

All chapters in this book have undergone peer review.

The Library of Congress Cataloging-in-Publication Data is available online at
http://catalog.loc.gov
LC record available at http://lccn.loc.gov/2018047560

ISSN 2542-9671
ISBN 978-90-04-39222-9 (paperback)
ISBN 978-90-04-39223-6 (hardback)
ISBN 978-90-04-39224-3 (e-book)

Copyright 2019 by Koninklijke Brill NV, Leiden, The Netherlands.
Koninklijke Brill NV incorporates the imprints Brill, Brill Hes & De Graaf,
Brill Nijhoff, Brill Rodopi, Brill Sense, Hotei Publishing, mentis Verlag,
Verlag Ferdinand Schöningh and Wilhelm Fink Verlag.
All rights reserved. No part of this publication may be reproduced, translated,
stored in a retrieval system, or transmitted in any form or by any means, electronic,
mechanical, photocopying, recording or otherwise, without prior written
permission from the publisher.
Authorization to photocopy items for internal or personal use is granted by
Koninklijke Brill NV provided that the appropriate fees are paid directly to The
Copyright Clearance Center, 222 Rosewood Drive, Suite 910, Danvers, MA 01923,
USA. Fees are subject to change.

This book is printed on acid-free paper and produced in a sustainable manner.

ADVANCE PRAISE FOR
WHO LOOK AT ME?!

"The Black queer body has been marginalized in education for far too long. When the Black queer body is seen, it is seen through a gaze that is rooted in anti-blackness. *Who Look at Me?!* is a book not only to shift the field, but our humanity. To see Black queer bodies wholeness and complexities at the same time. This book is a love poem of research addressed to the most vulnerable."
– Bettina L. Love, Associate Professor, University of Georgia, Department of Educational Theory & Practice

"Hill L. Waters (Durell M. Callier and Dominique C. Hill) are important and exciting emergent critical performance, queer and autoethnographic scholars, and this fierce and poetic text embodies their much-needed mission perfectly. As performance poets they draw on the rich histories of intersectional queer, performance and race scholarship in which Blackness, queerness and teacher-ness are performed as reciprocal and not mono-directional practices, seeing and being seen as deeply political work, co-constructing new worlds. This text shudders with not only the brilliance of these young authors, but also the seismic times in which it has been forged. Hill L. Waters challenge the teleologies and biases of education as a racist and homophobic network of communities, institutions, practices and as a sector. Here they reframe education as a set of events, of *intra-actions*, in order to suggest new worldings for doing what education has always promised (but mostly failed) to do: not just to see, but to recognise and raise up each student as a world of potentialities, and to fulfill our promise as teachers to nurture all students – and ourselves – as an ongoing co-constitutive liberatory pedagogical practice. Do yourself a favor and go buy this book now. Better yet, buy two and give one to a colleague or friend who needs it."
– Anne M. Harris, Associate Professor, Australian Research Council Future Fellow and RMIT University, Principal Research Fellow, School of Education and Digital Ethnography Research Centre

To Black youth in Baltimore, MD and Buffalo, NY,
who – in spite of being overseen and unseen and enduring
"terrible educations" – live out loud

CONTENTS

CONTENTS

ACKNOWLEDGEMENTS

The inception of this book begins in many places and at many times, but the spark was truly lit when our friend and mentor Ruth Nicole Brown asked us to locate our dot – the thing you would keep knowing even if the world didn't believe it. This book is a testament to our fundamental belief that Black girls and Black, queer lives matter. The tracing of that mattering is indebted to the courageous vision and continued wisdom offered in Brown's graduate seminar in 2014. Thank you. Equally so, we are thankful for the time and space shared with our fellow CritArtUers – colleagues and friends in the Critical Arts Based Research seminar – Tiffany Harris, Lisa Ortiz, the late Ashley C. Walls, Jessica Robinson, Taylor-Imani Linear, Aerian Brown, and Tarina Galloway.

Likewise, we are thankful to the collective care and Black girl celebration space of Saving Our Lives Hear Our Truths. Whether in digital, intentional, or analog form, our capacity to be fully human has grown because of each of you and with each encounter. This capacity is so fundamentally important. Thank you, Porshe Garner, Jessica Robinson, Cristina Carney-Richardson, Blair (DJ BE) Smith, and all the li'l homies with whom we have worked and "know and remember" through name, spirit, and SOLHOT collectivity. Equally, we are grateful for the space afforded during Black Girl Genius Week to co-create and meet other Black girls, organizers, and artists committed to centering art, performance, and collectivity to imagine new possibilities for living, loving, and being Black and still here.

For believers and practitioners of collectivity, this book has strewn across the pages, in the invisible smudge lines and hidden curriculum, the support, guidance, and careful critique offered by so many moments and people. Brittany Aronson, Ciara Lewis, Deanna Downes, and Ann Elizabeth Armstrong, thank you for the time and care you each gave to early chapter drafts. To Eric Darnell Pritchard, Alexis Pauline Gumbs, Brenda Nyandiko Sanya, our heartfelt gratitude always. Your presence in our lives and work has been sustenance. For your critical and supportive eyes, Aisha Durham and Chamara J. Kwakye, we are grateful. There's nothing like feedback from homegirls who helped grow you. The realness you bring is a gift, and it ensures that our words accomplish what we endeavor and that our spiritual and communal intentions are explicit and clear. Thank you.

As engaged, interdisciplinary scholar-artists, the International Congress of Qualitative Inquiry (ICQI) has been an especially important annual home-going to present, perform, and network. Through this home base, opportunities to workshop this project, share our scholarship, and benefit from an intellectual community were generously given and received. In particular, we met Amber Johnson and received a loving invitation to the Economies of Performance conference, witnessed the genius organizing and theorizing of Aisha Durham on the "Black feminist auto/ethnography" panel, alongside Cynthia Dillard, Mary E. Weems, Irma McClaurin, Maritza Quiñones, and Robin Boylorn. Each of these occasions deepened our care toward citational practice and emboldened our commitment to illuminating genealogies that place women of color, specifically Black feminist contributions to methodology, front and center. It is also at ICQI that we have immersed ourselves in the autoethnography special interest group organized by Stacy Holman Jones, which opened doors to being regular attendees of the Doing Autoethnography conference envisioned by Derek Bolen. At ICQI, we have met so many brilliant scholars who are generous with both time and heart. Kitrina Douglas, thank you for your commitment to "Qualitative Conversations," and for asking Hill L. Waters to take part in it. Thank you, Anne Harris and Kakali Bhattacharya for your solidarity and support.

Portions of this manuscript have benefitted from feedback from various intellectual communities, with sections of the study presented to audiences at the annual National Women's Studies conference, the American Educational Studies Association annual convening, the Imagining America annual convening, the Doing Autoethnography conference, Colgate University, University of Illinois at Urbana-Champaign, University of Missouri, and University of Alabama. A special thanks to Robin Boylorn for organizing the Discerning Diverse Voices Symposium, for which a portion of this study was performed. We have benefitted from questions, comments, and suggestions from audiences at each of these sites. This work would not be possible without the gracious funding of the Our Town grant from the National Endowment for the Arts, which was awarded to the Independent Media Center (IMC) and resulted in experiencing the creative genius (or prowess) of Lisa Faye of the Lisa Faye & Jeff Glassman Duo. Lisa you have always been and continue to be a gift, demonstrating the importance of artistic collaborations and the ability of art to actualize a world not yet here. Our time working with Lisa and the IMC was an invaluable opportunity to workshop and attain feedback on portions of research from this project. A special shout-out is owed to Blair E. Smith , the former IMC program coordinator, and to the youth participants who gave so willingly of their time, talent, and genius.

To Peter de Liefde, Shalen Lowell, Jolanda Karada, John Bennett, and all the wonderful people at Brill | Sense, thank you. Patricia Leavy, we are enormously grateful that you recognized our vision for this work as important and agreed to help bring it to light. The fact that you value creative freedom is a treasure. Your patience and steadfast support throughout this project is deeply appreciated. Katie Lowery, thank you for taking seriously our collective voice. Thank you for your attention to detail, honoring of our commitment to being a *we* with an *I* voice, and for punctuating our textual aesthetic. This book could not have been completed without you. Thank you to our research assistants, Martha Chauya and Jaclyn Chetty, for tracking down references and offering your critical thoughts and feedback about the work. To our colleagues in Educational Leadership at Miami University and in Black Studies at Amherst College, who have supported us and our interdisciplinary work from the beginning, we thank you.

Thank you to the artists, scholars, and artist-scholars cited throughout this book. You make our work possible. Our appreciation includes but is not limited to Ntozake Shange, Lorraine Hansberry, Nikky Finney, Alice Walker, Pat Parker, We Levitate, Tami Spry, Bryant Keith Alexander, Valerie Kinloch, Bettina Love, and Omi Osun Joni Jones. We are especially thankful to June Jordan. Our work owes much to her tenacity, foresight, and genius. Her book-length poem is a gift with many lessons, demonstrating the importance of relationships over rhetoric. Her commitment to friendship in carrying out the final wishes of her dear friend, Langston Hughes, was the spirit in which we too journeyed to ask again "who look," "who see." June, you are Black, alive, and looking back at us and we know it.

Understanding that time is non-linear and that we can work both in and outside of time, we know that this work is made possible by the traversing of spaces and encounters with strangers, family members, and loved ones. For your unwavering encouragement and belief in this project, your constant reminders that our work is important, and for your understanding, love, hugs, and when necessary, insistence that I take a break, Vanessa U. (Warrior) Bryant, you are *beyond* appreciated. For your energy, love, the joy you bring me, and your commitments to making this world a better place for all of us, Prentiss J. Haney, thank you. To our Village, both chosen and given family (in and beyond this plane) – Ms. Beverly Burwell; Mrs. Brenda Pinnick; BJ; Mary (Granny) Vance Boyd & the late Robert (Granddaddy Bobby) Boyd; the late Michael Antonio Boone (Uncle Mikey); Mama Crystal & the late

Twiggs (Poppy) Seymore tribe; Cynthia Tyson & Judy Alston (affectionately Madear & Padear); Aunties Kim, Debra, & CC; Esther (Denny) Smothers; Kim Heard-Boyland; the late Silvine (Gran) Bradford and Florence (Nang) Waters; Sheenan; Eddie; LaToya (li'l sis) Frazier; Nick; RJ; Reginald Underwood; our beloved parents, Silvine & Charles Dett, Natalie C. Brooks & the late Reginald Hill and Regina Bryant (Mama Gina), thank you all. To our nieces and nephews – Ayanna, Cobi, Daniel, Malic, Maleka, Noah, London, Ebony, Brittany, Mandie, and Carmelo – your youthful energy is an ever-present reminder of the necessity of this book. Thank you all, always, for your courageous love, assurance, the needed laughs, food, joy, and the gift of being seen. We hope to gift back to you that same abundance.

PROLOGUE

We are in our finest get-up gear. Me, in a bright peach, deep-plunge, cowl-neck t-shirt, short black shorts (a sure fail of the respectable fingertip test), and black cloth chucks. I want to be seen. She, servin' legs all day in a black sheer top, cobalt blue polyester extra-short shorts (what my granny would call hot pants), and five-inch floral heels.

As we proceed toward the vibrating bass, we take several pictures. To illuminate our melanin and get the fullness of our fits, we stage a photoshoot in the middle of Read Street, directly under a street light. Another longtime friend of mine, Toni, joins us, and we move our photo shoot into the alley alongside the club.

The night air is thick, filled with a mixture of city smells, asphalt, weed, and alcohol, accented with our cologne and perfume. I am wearing Polo Blue, the scent that always gets me noticed. She is out in these streets to hit the dance floor. So although being noticed isn't necessarily on her list, she adorns her wrists, behind her ears, and across her belly with Fiori by Vince Camuto.

It is a typical summer night in Baltimore, just the right humidity that folks can either be inside or outside depending on whether or not they have air units in their home. We walk up to Hippo[1] and wait in a short line (no more than six people ahead of us). The kids have come to play. Only two security guards and a crew consisting mostly of Black studs stand between us and our moment of catching the "Spirit in the Dark."[2] The night unfolds as usual. We enter to the left, passing another security guard. After we pay our cover, we follow the short, black hallway that leads to the rectangular dance floor. There are three levels to this part of the club – a small, shadowed set of booths and two dance levels that resemble a roller skating rink. The outer ring, covered in carpet, is mostly used for walking, cruising, ordering drinks at the bars, and socializing. The lower oval floor is made of wood, with two freestanding floor speakers on each side of the dance floor. They tower over Toni, who is almost six feet tall, and add an extra dance platform for the adventurous. The sound of Baltimore Club vibrates, ricocheting off the black walls, filling up every cavity of our being.

As the night progresses, Toni needs to go to the restroom. I accompany him, because as a general rule you never let your Judy go alone, whether to relieve ourselves, preen in the mirror, or strut across the room. While

I wait in the hallway for Toni to emerge from the restroom, a police officer approaches me, stating that I cannot block the hallway. I explain that I am simply waiting for a friend, but he insists that I cannot stand in the hallway and waits for me to leave. I am unnerved, and write the following, "Today I was accosted by a Black police officer in a gay club, essentially telling me I could not stand in a hallway to wait for a friend. I think he's straight and I'm tired of being policed like this, I also feel some type of way as we die like this" (D. Callier, personal communication, July 31, 2015).

Earlier that summer, at the same club, I wrote, "Four police cars and only three officers noted today, but the club is closing soon" (D. Callier, personal communication, June 19, 2015). I can recall taking note of the police officers within the club space for over a year. As someone who frequented this club often, or as often as afforded, the police presence was particularly salient. Baltimore is always home, but I am a bit of an interloper and have not lived there for 10 years now. The first time I returned home and noticed the police officers in the club on "hip-hop night," I was alarmed. The club had gone through several phases during my queer club-going years, including the sudden end of hip-hop night, a resurgence of the night, and then the introduction of a police presence inside and eventually outside of the club.

In writing the aforementioned memory, we were struck by how sense is made and mapped upon bodies. For instance, when trying to describe the group of assumed Black lesbian women in front of us at the club, we considered the variety of ways that the group is described and understood by outsiders to the community and by those of us within the community. Should we have characterized them as identifying or presenting as studs? Masculine of center? Are these the same ascriptions they would use to self-identify, given the interplay of gender and sexuality that are often present within queer communities? Such categorization becomes particularly troubled when we consider race, class, and how Blackness configures and confounds classifications along gender and sexuality spectrums. We were also struck by our differing reactions to the surveillance of our bodies. For instance, in Buffalo, New York, Hill's hometown, the police are usually seen posted outside a club, standing in the breezeway leading to the club, and circling the block where the Black gay club (when it was open) is located. She was unbothered by the police presence but took notice and gave side eye to the officer inside, who patted her down with his stare.

We begin here with a memory of surveillance to illuminate the myriad of angles in which gaze is directed, as well as its effect. This leads us to the development of this text and our historic and contemporary oscillation with the function, creation, distortion, and reimagining of the gaze onto and emanating from Black bodies. Here, body is multifaceted, from the singular Black body to its collective imagining and needs, to the Black body situated as queer, as youthful, as girl, woman, memory, and possibility. Before continuing to expose and make ourselves vulnerable for the purpose of better understanding, critiquing, and problematizing (your/our) gaze of Black, queer bodies, there are some things we need you to know.

Reading this text makes you a read(er). There are a multitude of levels and approaches to reading. Here, you are more than a reader, one who absorbs the words and articulations offered on a page. Instead, you are a read(er). Let us explain.

Taking cues from Black, queer expressive culture, our usage of read(er) registers on various scales. Read(er) as verb, engaged in the act of reading various texts (e.g., bodies, visual images, and literary texts). Read(er) as noun, to be a subject made visible within and through community, vis-à-vis practices of reading. Read(er) as adjective, a way to describe. Each of these ways of reading – to understand, to describe, as an art form, as play, as being read – hinges upon engagements with the Black, queer cultural practices of being read/reading.

In the words of Dorian Corey, "Shade comes from reading. Reading came first" (Livingston, 1990). Important here is Corey's invocation and education. Within this text, we take seriously the art of shade and the art of reading as forms of Black, queer expressive culture that mediate ways to see and be seen within white, heteronormative society. As Corey goes on to state, "Reading is the real art form of insult. You get in a smart crack, and everyone laughs and kikis because you've found a flaw and exaggerated it, then you've got a good read going." Corey was a prominent drag queen performer, designer, and house mother of House Corey. Featured in Jennie Livingston's 1990 documentary on the drag scene in New York City, *Paris is Burning*, Corey's words and figure looms large, and her words are still quoted and important today. What we wish to highlight here is that Corey's description of reading and shade sets up the interplay of the act, of being seen and seeing within a community of love, vulnerability, and survival.

The practice and usage of shade and reading flips power on its head (even if just temporarily) and is sometimes utilized as a means of finding and creating community, shielding those within the community from the outside world, and offering different readings and assessments of their bodies, values, and valuation. Located within Black, queer expressive culture and Black girlhood, our reading practice takes its cues from Zebra Katz's

"Ima Read" (featuring Njena Reddd Foxxx), Dorian Corey's ruminations on the art of shade and reading, and June Jordan's textual eye. Within this bounded community, reading is done with precision and within context. Contextual readings within community allow for ways to read – to see – Black bodies and Black, queer bodies, not from historical tropes but rather from community, in loving relationship, and on our own terms. To read is to read right. To be a read(er) is to read within this literary tradition.

Taken together, you as a read(er) embark upon literacy, curriculum building, and theorizing, made within and through Black and queer bodies and communities. For some of you, this means you are seeing yourself reflected back to you, while others may stand on the peripheries of the communities centered here. Herein lies the challenge of reorienting ourselves toward one another. Thus, our turn to gaze is an invitation to reorient accountability for what occurs when we see one another and insists that education require those looking *at* bodies – especially those bodies non-white, non-binary, non-male, and overall non-dominant – take in the history, culture, and politics embedded in their gaze.

Who Look at Me?! is relational and ethics centered. As Black, queer scholar-artists in academe, colleagues, and graduates of the same doctoral program with similar training, as friends mistaken for romantic lovers (we aren't sure why), as graduates of free lunches, we wrote this book to posit Black queerness as a way of seeing, and to render more visible the interplay of Blackness, queerness, education, and performance. This book is contestation and response to being disappeared, fragmented, surveilled, and made to watch bodies, Blackness, sexuality, and their contentious relationships be erased, sterilized (in discourse) and dipped in a new color of paint, policed, and placed in opposing corners. Taking grave issue with erasure and remaining more interested in Black queerness as a prolific sight to gaze at and through, we offer collective auto/ethnography as a technology for identifying blind spots in the levels of gaze directed at our bodies – Black, queer bodies. Moreover, we offer ourselves reflexively and in conversation with one another as a site of critique, knowledge, and possibility.

With collective work comes additional labor. While doing this work and completing this manuscript, we have been met with similar yet nagging questions. How does this count? How will this count? These questions, if taken front row, might have discouraged us from writing this text. And yet, here we are. Still, we deliberated whether the time was right to write this text, particularly against a backdrop of suspicion for this kind of work. Work that is experimental disrupts standards of professionalism and/or challenges the ways in which promotion, tenure, and evaluative practices and policies seek to count and quantify our labor (Brown, Carducci, & Kuby, 2014). Single author or co-author work is widely accepted, but collective authorship? Collective scholarship?

Our coming together was and remains intentional. Since deciding to write together, we have learned a great deal about each other, supported and challenged one another on how we engage with academia and institutional expectations, and reflected deeply upon our collective practice. This practice is rooted in feminist, lesbian, and queer-of-color collectives, which serve as important bedrocks for a variety of academic disciplines and are the wellspring from which methodological and theoretical frameworks were born. The joys of working in collectivity versus collaboration prove intense and necessary. We realize that collaborations usually offer clearly defined beginnings and endings, yet we seek to continue. Despite its intent of togetherness, collaboration often takes the form of lone creating and writing with a piecing together of individual creations, whereas we wrote this virtually, face-to-face, live via Google Doc, *together*.

We would be remiss, however, if we didn't acknowledge that our deliberations around how to write together as well as the choice to write requires intense labor, communication, and is not without consequences (seen and not yet materialized) or barriers to organizing ourselves within and through collectivity (Brown, 2013). Despite these challenges, and perhaps in spite of them, we persist as a collective.

When the reading is done (here), there will be more reading to do. We endeavor, however, to leave you with a wider field of vision, new ways to think about how to see Blackness and Black people, and a growing ability to take responsibility for the systems, people, and things your gaze recognizes, occludes, and misrecognizes.

In this moment, be open. Take joy in looking at Black bodies, Black stories, Black, queer bodily stories. We are here to be seen, but on our own terms. Embrace and assume responsibility for your gaze. Give your gaze permission to take on the form of browsing, rubbernecking, gawking, and/or peek-a-booing. We see you looking. We see you, read(er). We see you looking and reading us.

NOTES

[1] Opening in 1972, The Hippo was one of several gay bars/establishments in Baltimore (Rector & Gorelick, 2015). The club was recently sold to make way for a CVS by longtime owner, Charles L. "Chuck" Bowers (Rector & Gorelick, 2015). A queer social space,

The Hippo maintains collective and individual queer memory. Collective memories of the space include the usage of the space to provide support to gay men who contracted AIDS during the 1980s, as well as a variety of other altruistic means for LGBTQ persons within Baltimore. Those collective memories of kinship and care also envelop individual memories, like that of my own and my close network of friends. Although The Hippo is the memory shared here, three mainstay gay nightlife places have closed over the last decade, The Paradox, The Hippo, and Grand Central. The importance of intergenerational queer spaces and their absence or forced removal has been taken up within recent queer studies scholarship (Hardt, 2013; Holmes, 2011).

[2] See Johnson (1998), referencing the sacred/secular space the Black gay club creates for Black, queer communities, a reveling in the Black, queer body in ecstasy and on display, and Aretha Franklin's song of the same title.

WHY AUTO/ETHNOGRAPHY EDUCATION AND PERFORMANCE NOW

November 2016, I am traveling to Canada. Preparing to engage in conversations about feminism and decoloniality in the now, I am able to momentarily escape the surreal reality of the departure of our first elected Black president looming on the horizon and his soon-to-be successor. Making sense of the reality of our increased awareness of violence faced by Black bodies and queer bodies, I receive an email from a student in my course on Critical Youth Studies. The email is filled with fear and anxiety. The student informs me that due to the outcome of the election and the growing tensions on campus, he did not feel safe leaving his house to turn in a take-home quiz. He goes on to express that given the history of violence and intimidation on our campus, coupled with his own sense of anxiety, he did not feel that his presence on campus was warranted, safe, or would foster any learning. As I digest his email, I wonder, does he not see me, my Black, queer self, as someone just as vulnerable as he is to facing and enduring violence in this town and on this campus? Seeing a teachable moment, wanting to be seen, and hoping to create an opportunity for empathy, I respond to the student. I share here verbatim my response in full:

Greetings Nick,[1]

Thank you for your message. Today, I am at a loss for words as I am made to reflect on our contemporary moment and my continued role, especially now, as an educator.

I want to share a story with you. The year is 2004. I, along with several of my friends from high school, just drove over eight hours to a town called Oxford, Ohio. We are here as a small representation of Black and progressive folks, mostly students, from Baltimore City, who have been organizing for our right to an adequate education. We are tutors, organizers, sons, daughters, friends, and lovers, traveling to join in a celebration for the 40th reunion of Freedom Summer. I did not know then what Freedom Summer was, why it was important, or who Bob Moses really was other than the founder of the Algebra Project.

© KONINKLIJKE BRILL NV, LEIDEN, 2019 | DOI:10.1163/9789004392243_001

We are one of the many legs of this project, but as young people who know our history but not always the specificity of it, the moment we are participating in loses a specific importance, despite our knowing deeply that we are traveling for something big.

The weekend is filled with spiritually moving speeches by John Lewis, who shakes our hands and eagerly congratulates us for our work in Baltimore. We spend the weekend learning about parts of our history as Black folk that we knew but didn't know. Remembering Chaney, Schwerner, and Goodman. Feeling our new sense of freedom as a mixture of high school students and a few first-generation college students. Later in the day, we are joined by Black students from Miami University who are charged with showing us around town. The campus is beautiful. We pass a row of fraternity houses; students are partying. I feel safe *enough*. We feel safe *enough*. We continue our tour, approaching the campus bars that are bustling with a type of social life I had never witnessed before. "Nigger!" Sailing across the wind, landing somewhere on our backs, in our laps, upon our ears, "Nigger bitch."

A sea of rosy white faces and blonde hair moves indiscriminately across the backdrop of the alleyway. We know the direction of the assault but not [the assailant]. Our tour guides turn to us, "Yeah, that happens sometimes. We just ignore 'em." This is my first time leaving Baltimore, a very Black city with a very Black school system. I attend a predominately white university with a Black president. I have known Black women principals, Black male janitors, and white lesbian assistant principals. Dr. Jay, a Jewish man, is the reason I am, we are, here. In all of my 18 years, I have never known this thing that I thought was somewhere out there, somewhere maybe in the past, somewhere safely away from me. We turn to each other, exchange looks, and begin to walk back to our rooms.

I share this story with you to illustrate that I am well aware of the histories of violence which congeal in Oxford, at Miami, and for which bodies like mine are made to bear. *The story is my story, and despite that experience, I actively chose to come and teach here at Miami.* With this backdrop, I rarely (if ever) feel safe in Oxford, at Miami University, in my own classroom.

I wish I had words that might comfort you to assure you of your safety, but absent of this promise, what I can say is that I am, have been, and continue to work toward freedom and creating a more just world. It is what we have been practicing this semester in stretching our thinking, relating the course materials back to our lives, and providing ourselves opportunities to engage with each other in ways that are atypical for "student/teacher" dynamics.

I have no words to allay your fears or anxieties. What I can do is to respond to you and let you know that I hear you. Take care of yourself. I will accept your electronic quiz, but will only grade the hard copy, which I will accept from you in class on Monday. See you on Monday!

In peace,

–

Durell M. Callier, Ph.D.
Assistant Professor
Cultural Studies and Curriculum
Department of Educational Leadership
Miami University

I offer my exchange with the student to pose a series of questions related to education in this moment, how we see or don't see each other as teachers, students, and co-learners, and in particular, how Blackness is obfuscated in these educational moments of (mis)recognition. Hailed as a "nigger" in the memory, I am seen, right? A decade later, now a faculty member at the institution in which the racially violent memory is staged, and forcibly re-lived as I am made to recount the memory to be seen by my white, queer student, but am I seen? Is violence the site at which objects are made known? Where and when do objects become subjects, move to being placed into sight as fully human? I am not an object, right? Are we speaking to each other as subjects to subjects, people to people? How are our educational practices complicit in seeing and not seeing Blackness, that is, Black students, Black educators, Black communities? What happens when we are misrecognized? What remedies exist to our issues of sight? These questions fundamentally sit at the crux of the children's book by June Jordan, *Who Look at Me* (1969), which inspires our title and our research on locating Blackness, queerness, and the body as sites of knowledge and curriculum to shift education.

FRAMING SHIFTING THE GAZE

In elementary school, my mom entered a lottery to land a place for me in a magnet school. At a young age, I knew I wanted to go to college. In seventh grade, teachers and mentors told me that to attend an elite college required graduating from a prestigious high school. Mentors and adults in the non-formal educational spaces I attended (i.e., church, after-school programs, and Girl Scouts) encouraged me to seek ways to enhance my chances for success. My family was working class. On the recommendation of a friend, I applied to an enrichment program, Buffalo Prep, designed to assist talented inner-city youth in their pursuit of academic success. I forfeited the summers before eighth and ninth grade to participate in accelerated courses in English, math, and science, applied to mostly private high schools, and eventually attended an all-girls Catholic high school.

As a youth with ambition, I saw each of these educational experiences as opportunities to reach my ultimate goal: college. I sensed the unfairness of the obstacles endured by people who come from the inner city, like myself. Equally, I intuited no reward for seeing something others surely saw. I became an anomaly, a gift, an example. I did not know to ask these questions at the time, but now I frequently ruminate and push my students to examine: What is education and where does it take place? What teaching/learning spaces assume Blackness to be a marker of cultural wealth? Once I have graduated and received the degrees, what should my relationship to myself be?

Who Look at Me?!: Shifting the Gaze of Education through Blackness, Queerness, and the Body takes up questions of sight, seeing, and the negation of seeing the Black, queer body, its erasure in education. "Erasure is violence," and the erasures of which we are interested are those of slight, misrecognition, and nonrecognition in how we look at, away from, and see Blackness (Fleetwood, 2011; Morris, 2016). Specifically, we explore the sorts of blind spots and erasures which are epistemic and ontological in nature, informing our education system and educational practice in the United States, a system which erases the histories of Black children, their innate genius, and the communities in which they reside and come from, and diminishes them and the attributes of their communities to stereotypes of poverty (Emdin, 2012; Love, 2014).

Looking is subjective (Brown et al., 2014; Fleetwood, 2011; Hill, 2017). Narratives constructed thereafter are inevitably political. Moreover, to gaze is a communicative process between the gazer and the object in view, steeped in history and culture. In relationship, then, it follows that accountability should be shared between and across the two. However, this is not so, especially as it pertains to non-white, non-binary, non-male, and other bodies marked by socially constructed norms as non-dominant. Bodies inhabiting non-dominant identities become cast as abnormal and even deviant (Cacho, 2007; Cohen, 2004).

Over time, the gaze from people with dominant identities onto those with non-dominant ones creates narratives that evolve into definitive and static constructions. Canadian Black feminist Katherine McKittrick (2006) notes the inconvenient work of Black bodies in particular:

> But this geographic work – acknowledging the real and the possible, mapping the deep poetics of Black landscapes – is also painful work. The site of memory is also the *sight* of memory – imagination requires a return to and engagement with painful places, worlds where Black people were and are denied humanity, belonging, and formal citizenship; this means a writing of where and how Black people occupy space through different forms of violence and disavowal. (p. 33)

McKittrick's articulation frames Blackness as a diasporic landscape traversing space and time. As such, individual Black bodies help to create, maintain, and shift Blackness. Moreover, she stitches together the location of memory and injury (the body) with the possibility of healing (the sight). Implicit in this understanding is that *seeing* is vital to the processes of doing harm and inciting healing. Thereby, our turn to gaze is invocation to redistribute accountability for what is engendered from gazing and insist that education require those looking at bodies, especially those bodies non-white, non-binary, non-male, and overall situated as non-dominant, must reconcile the history, culture, and politics embedded in their gaze.

Implicit in McKittrick's assertion of the body as both a place where harm is enacted and a tool for transmuting (though not necessarily undoing) enmity is the work necessary to seeing the body anew. Supporting McKittrick's articulation of the body as a multi-dimensional space, I argue that the body is best understood "as a dynamic, haunted entity, contextually understood with physical, discursive, individual, and collective manifestations" (Hill, 2018, p. 386). Similarly, we understand the processes of being seen and seeing as a parallel enterprise. For example, how Black students in formal educational spaces are seen is contingent upon the "eye" and "I" of the gazer. The eye here refers to the visuality of a person and what they can see literally, while the I accounts for who this person is and their personal, political, and identity proximal to who they are gazing upon. Reflecting upon the productive uses of autoethnography to draw out the layers of identity and subjectivity, Tami Spry (2011) articulates, "…[U]sing autoethnography as a method of inquiry inherently sets the subject in the context of her own multiple, heterogeneous, unstable identities where "I" is always and already constituted through a variety of "we" (p. 53). Extending and distinct from the performative I disposition, the eye and I implore that educators, teachers, educational researchers, and others with power and position in the lives of Black youth especially, develop a keen awareness of the ingredients of their eyes and I's.

THE ORIGINS OF SHIFTING THE GAZE IN OUR WORK

We are both students of Saving Our Lives Hear Our Truths[2] (SOLHOT). For us, our coming to and sustained engagement with SOLHOT marked a shift in how we saw the world, each other, Black youth, specifically Black girls, and knowledge production, as well as what constitutes education and educational research. Unlearning was (and remains) central to the labor of working with Black girls in ways that situate them as knowledge producers and experts on theorizing and articulating meaning of their experience. In SOLHOT, we had to first reckon with the baggage we brought to seeing and relating to Black girls. Individually and in collectivity, we turned the lens onto ourselves through organizing meetings, SOLHOT sessions, and classes created to further understand the epistemological groundings of this cultural work Ruth Nicole Brown (2009) named SOLHOT and Black girlhood celebration. Unknowingly then, Black girls and Black girlhood as an organizing construct was teaching us the imperative of self-reflexivity and hipping us to the mechanics and ethics of auto/ethnography. In different but always impactful ways, our time in SOLHOT presented subtle and less subtle opportunities to choose what type of scholars we would become and what aesthetics would accompany those deliberations.

She asked us, "How did you come to do performance as part of your research?"[3] The previous night, we had concluded our performance of SOLHOT: The Mixtape Remix, a collectively written, performance ethnography that reflected our work with the girls of SOLHOT[4] and offered up salient critiques of the systems of inequality that limit our collective right to life. Dr. Brown (or Dr. B as we affectionately call her) was up to her usual, class was always in session and we were about to learn a lesson. This was a part of our routine, teacher turned student, student turned teacher. This was our opportunity to say what we knew; she always believed (often before we knew ourselves) that we indeed knew something, something everybody else also needed to know. Her prodding, guidance, belief, and support were necessary, necessary because schooling and disciplinary training had divorced us from our own sources of power and knowledge. And so here she was, like Toni Cade Bambara, reminding us of the need to share what we knew within a collective, because "if your friends don't know it, then you don't know it" (Bambara, 2009).

When we shared, I was often surprised by our answers, by our collective genius, and not because I did not think we were geniuses but because I spent a lot of time pretending that this was not the case. Pretending not to know was costly, but it had become a defense against classrooms, hallway meetings with peers, and conference spaces which asked the same question, "How did you come to do performance as a part of your research," but with less sincerity and care than Dr. B had used. The real question implied by their tone was, "How is that research?" As Ruth Nicole Brown (2013) notes, "Research that is creative, public, and grounded in collaboration with marginalized communities, conducted by scholars of color, is always and already suspect" (p. 31). Aware of this, I often pretended not to know, but this time I would not be able to get off the hook.

> When I answered the question, I often said, that it was born from need. In some of my earlier graduate school writing, I frequently included a poem, song lyrics, or something from a childhood cartoon that I thought was relevant to the literature. Whenever I was writing for a class, I never wrote a formal paper, sitting and searching. I think I'm still trying to forge connections because in trying to name exactly what I do, I remember how central my spiritual upbringing has been to my work. There's something in my work that I would identify as a calling but haven't fully owned. (D. Callier, personal communication, February 10, 2012)

In Disrupting Qualitative Inquiry: Possibilities and Tensions in Educational Research, Brown et al. (2014) identified the need for a shift in educational research specifically, and qualitative research broadly. They call for a need to "engage in methodological advocacy, calling attention to the new forms of knowledge and social change made possible by embracing a wider repertoire of method(ologie)s than are currently acknowledged by the disciplinary powers that be" (p. 4). In locating the need for disruptive inquiries in educational research, they identified their own paradigmatic shifts in coming to disruptive inquiry as/in educational research, and in being educational researchers and professors. Embracing this call for the need for disruptive qualitative educational research and sharing similar stories of disruption, we have offered our stories to serve as both narratives of disruption and stories that highlight the when, where, how, and why of shifting the gaze in education. This shift, this disruption in the status quo, is important to how we come to do research, the inherent beliefs carried out and mapped onto our research endeavors, and the development of educational researchers and practitioners.

Furthermore, it highlights the possibilities often foreclosed by disciplining regimes which "perpetuate the inequitable status quo in our schools and communities" (Brown et al., 2014, p. 2) through the gazes characterized by the domination of positivist and constructivist discourses and assumptions of valued ways of knowing (epistemology), data collection, analysis, and representation (methodology), and the very nature of our shared reality (ontology) (Pasque, Carducci, Kuntz, & Gildersleeve, 2012). Building from this work, we seek to shift the gaze in educational research and praxis, and propose the usage of methodological and pedagogical innovation broadly, and specifically through performance autoethnography.

SHIFTING THE EDUCATIONAL GAZE NOW: INSISTING ON PEDAGOGIES OF FREEDOM, CREATIVITY, AND PRAXIS

The tempering sweetness
of a little girl who wears
her first pair of earrings
and a red dress
the grace of a boy removing
a white mask he makes beautiful (Jordan, 1969, p. 7)

I am
impossible to explain
remote from old and new interpretations
and yet
not exactly (Jordan, 1969, p. 17)

In 1969, June Jordan published a children's book, *Who Look at Me*. As a book-length poem accompanied by a mixture of fine art portraits, images, and illustrations, the text takes seriously the liminal space of childhood and adulthood that Black children often traverse. Although written for a younger audience, Jordan's text, makes plain that because of the ways Blackness is read, Black youth-filled bodies are read as "wrong" beginning early in childhood (Jordan, 2005). Through rich and vivid details, she utilizes Black vernacular, art, and poetry to render complex depictions of Black life. In doing so, Jordan stages a conversation that depicts the complexity of Black American life while also reflecting and critiquing American society and culture in general.

The title of our book pays homage to Jordan because of the two simple yet profound questions her poem asks, then and now: "Who look at me?" and

"Who see?" (Jordan, 1969, p. 7). These questions are cautionary statements as well as an admonishment to the gaze upon which Black (youth) bodies are (not) seen within American society. Rhetorical in nature, these questions demand read(er)s to be reflexive and then move toward action. It is important to note that one of the lessons of the text is applicable to adults, although adults are not Jordan's primary audience. She takes seriously children's ability to understand the world in which they live, to be critical consumers of various media forms, and to dialogically interact with the text and spin their own insights, theories, and meanings from the poem and its accompanying pictures.

The fact that *Who Look at Me* is a book-length poem should not be missed. As Black woman poets have demonstrated, good poetry has the ability to do "something" within the world – it is capable of producing a sustainable revolution that values human life. Our profound belief in poetry's utility rests on a cultural legacy of Black, queer women and men who have utilized poetry as a means to preserve culture, incite change, educate, and create critical consciousness while offering solace and critique to systems of racialized, sexualized, and gendered forms of oppression (Beam, 1986; Harris, 2005; Jordan, 1969, 1985; Byrd, Cole, & Guy-Sheftall, 2009; Muller & The Poetry for the People Blueprint Collective, 1995; Shange, 1977). A political tool, poetry serves as a means to understand the self, reflect culture, and challenge hegemony. Poetry stages an intervention onto the gaze that would seek to imagine Black bodies as wrong, already dead, or dying. These interventions, the utility of poetry, and more broadly, the creative sit at the crux of this book.

These two questions, "Who look at me" and "Who see," provide a dialectic conversation in which the false dichotomy of adulthood and childhood for Black Americans explodes, asking both child and parent, teacher and educator, adults and youth, to consider how they internally and externally look at Black people in particular, youth especially, and each other in general.

Setting the stage for a relevant reading of then and now, past, present, and future, Jordan's literary text/children's book/hybrid poem continuously challenges read(er)s to ask themselves and society as a whole who sees Black people, thus inviting the read(er) to see Black culture differently. This is illustrated in the above quote with regards to seeing the "tempering sweetness of a little girl" and the "grace of a boy" (Jordan, 1969, p. 7). Jordan also answers her question with a response that points to mystery and a shaded understanding, rather than a finite and clear picture of the subject(s) within the poem. Both the questions and answers presented within the poem are highlighted here because of their concern with how we see marginalized people and cultures, especially Black culture. Further, these questions create a central locus at which to ask important questions regarding often distinctly held fields that we bring together in our practice as an artist-scholar collective, Hill L. Waters, our theorization on Black, queer life, and throughout this book. In particular, *Who Look at Me?!* sutures together the fields and critical methodologies of cultural studies of education, Black studies, Black queer studies, performance studies, and autoethnography. Further it asks us to consider how we see Black people and Black youth, complexly and wholly. While also examining how we see their lived experiences as sites of knowledge, which shifts how we might think about education broadly.

Shifting the gaze poses unique opportunities to the aforementioned disciplinary fields through our creative endeavors as an auto/ethnographic performance collective. As critical auto/ethnographers, our slash is in alignment with other Black woman scholars who utilize the slash as a way to signify and testify to the collective embedded within the individual (Boylorn, 2013b; Weems, personal communication, May 9, 2012). Auto/ethnography articulates a practice committed to more than the lone autoethnographer; rather, the auto/ethnographer exists in community, collaboratively writing a text, speaking with and to a community, often exploring multiple intersectional communities' experiences, reflecting them back to that community and illuminating the lived experience, needs, and desires of an ignored people to the rest of society. As part of an emergent genre of research and writing practices, collaborative research writing (duoethnography) and collaborative autoethnography acknowledge the ways in which identity shapes experience and perspective. Therefore, collaboration in the research process is an attempt to collect and represent a more holistic portrait of a given phenomenon and/or culture (Angrosino, 2008; Alexander, Moreira, & Kumar, 2012; Denzin, Lincoln, & Smith, 2008; Kasl & Yorks, 2010; Richardson & St. Pierre, 2008; Weems, Callier, & Boylorn, 2014; Wyatt, Gale, Russell, Pelias, & Spry, 2011). Hill L. Waters contributes to and extends these practices in an effort to think about the possibility of collaborative auto/ethnography as an experimental methodological practice, political commitment, and enactment of love, justice, and hope. By offering up our life experiences as a means of insertion (not to speak for an entire community, but to speak to our experiences), it is our hope that other Black and queer persons will find moments of resonance and recognition within our narratives (Boylorn, 2013b).

At the root of our collaboration is the infusion of performance-based methodologies, inclusive of poetry, theater, and dance. Each of these genres, when utilized as a political tool and as a means to understand the self, reflect culture, and challenge hegemony, become useful tools for educational praxis, research, and qualitative researchers. It is within this space that "identity is no longer a transcendental or essential self that is revealed, but a 'staging of subjectivity' – a representation of the self as a performance [...] The subject 'in history' is rendered destabilized and incoherent, a site of discursive pressures and articulations" (Russell, 1999, p. 276). Blending the two – performance and auto/ethnography – we seek to illuminate the possibilities of critical collaborative auto/ethnography, which at times utilizes performance to visibly make salient and therefore confront racialized, gendered, and sexed corporeal cartographies (McKittrick & Woods, 2007), as well as provide transformative and subversive enactments of social justice (Denzin & Lincoln, 2008; Spry, 2001).

TOOLS TO ENGENDER GAZE SHIFTING

To read Blackness and queerness anew, in education specifically, we offer two particular tools: performance and auto/ethnography.

Performance is a contested term and is taken up across this book to be defined as theory, method, and event. Specifically, we deploy performance in its multiplicity as a discursive space uniting theory and praxis, as a method of inquiry providing entryways into the narratives of marginalized individuals/communities, and as the play of imagination, the contesting of rigid notions of identity and community boundaries while exploring the richness of what is and what can be through embodied habits and dramatic forms (Carlson, 1996; Denzin, 2003; hooks, 1990; Johnson, 2006; Madison & Hamera, 2006). Moving beyond the mimetic or theatrical, performance theory serves as a framework within this project to provide concrete applications, aesthetics, politics, and ways of comprehending how human beings fundamentally make culture, affect power, and reinvent their ways of being in the world (Madison & Hamera, 2006). Situated in the everyday cultural milieu of Black life, performance provides insights into understanding, theorizing, and illuminating lived experience against the backdrops of power, politics, and pedagogy. Shifting the gaze in education is to attend to the types of knowledge, which might be learned through enfleshened knowledge and pedagogy. Attuning the field of education toward performance pedagogy creates the possibility, as Alexander (2006a) describes, for a "performance studies paradigm of pedagogy" in which traditional forms of knowing, teaching, knowledge production, and social systems are interrogated, challenged, and transformed in order "to liberate the human spirit" (p. 253).

Engagement with performance is an act of critical pedagogy, which situates our bodies, our stories, and the communities we love and represent as central figures of analysis and knowledge creation.

Autoethnography intentionally makes room for exploring dialectics between bodies, cultures, histories, and the self. As an ethically grounded methodology (Lapadat, 2018), it assumes sight and thereby meaning is partial, socially and culturally mediated, and power-laden. To counter positivist ideologies that deny even the plausibility of the aforementioned reality, autoethnography shifts the attention from culture itself to how the researcher interacts in, responds to, and experiences culture(s) (Holman Jones, Adams, & Ellis, 2013). As a methodology intended to illuminate the self, culture, and meaning as interlaced, autoethnography is a "doubled storytelling form and moves from self to culture and back again" (Boylorn, 2013a, p. 174). Undergirding reflexivity, a key tool for conducting research and crafting autoethnographic writing, is the ability to create sensorial representations that urge read(er)s to engage reading as a personal, political action. To compel a read(er), the representational choice, and by extension the research, must be visceral and evoking. Said differently, "Understanding research as embodied creativity – making things with our bodies – opens up possibilities for understanding research not just as abstractions (although abstractions have much to offer, too), but as material actions and material consequences" (Ellingson, 2017, p. 191). Autoethnography, then, creates a pathway for seeing the self, specifically our sight (gaze) afforded upon culture(s) and others as having tangible consequences.

As an analytic, BlackQueer is deployed as a means to think through how Blackness is perceived as non-normative and the impacts of this understanding mapped onto Black people, culture, and customs (Callier, 2018). The conjoining of the words Black and queer on the page denotes an intentional language shift to explore how Blackness, and thus Black people, have been queered by the state. In each chapter, we inspect the various gazes that have constricted understandings of the possibilities of Black lives, and demonstrate how Black heterosexuals and their non-heterosexual peers have queer relationships with that state. This line of inquiry seeks to queer educational and curriculum studies, builds upon the important works of Somerville (2000), Cohen (1997, 2010), Spillers (1987), and Holland (2000), and pays close attention to how processes of racialization in the United States have come to view Black subjectivity as "unintelligible, aberrant, excessive, beyond acceptable heteronormative machinations of productivity and utility – Blackqueer" (Callier, 2008, p. 29). Such methodological, epistemological, and theoretical frames within the text help us to further take up the charge of Nicole Fleetwood (2011), in which we "return to what we already know with curiosity and openness so that new forms of knowing and recognition emerge" (p. 7). Said differently, how can we look anew at ourselves, each other, and Black youth when their bodies, culture, and genius and our own are refracted in an educational kaleidoscope (both within and outside of schools) as the image, view, and viewer shifts?

When power and gaze converge in the absence of critical reflexivity, they reproduce the status quo, embolden hierarchical structures and metanarratives, and generate tropes and archetypes. As critical auto/ethnographers, our work takes a vested interest in attuning to power and inequity while cultivating space for those voices, knowledge, and experiences otherwise silenced and/ or undermined. While our work emanates from a Black feminist genealogy, where the collective is embedded within the individual (Weems, personal communication, May 9, 2012), and indicated textually with a slash between auto and ethnography, in this text, to account for the various histories and genealogical tracings possible within this methodology, we use auto/ ethnography and autoethnography interchangeably.

Hill L. Waters contributes to this methodological work and extends its reach by explicitly inserting Blackness and Blackqueer as analytical frames and spirit into collaborative autoethnography genealogies. Collaborative auto/ethnography for us, within this project specifically, serves as a vital tool for bringing the artistic inquiry and analytics initially presented by Jordan (1969). Initially started by the late Langston Hughes and later completed by June Jordan (Kinloch, 2006), *Who Look at Me* serves as a starting point to consider gaze as an analytic on conversations related to race, anti-Black racism, and living in and under racialized gazes. Similarly, our aim is to continue the work of these Black and queer cultural workers by advancing this particularly Black feminist analytic to consider the reading of Blackness, and queerness in education. Equally important, is the possibility of generating new visions of Blackness by interfacing with artistic methods and analyses rooted in the creative (Brown 2013).

AUTOETHNOGRAPHY AND EDUCATION

Autoethnography's traction in education is novel and tenuous. Elucidated more in Chapter 4, "Answering the Call: Centering Spirit in Auto/ Ethnography," autoethnography's utility in education is muddled by positivist residue. As Hughes, Pennington, and Makris (2012) highlight, the resistance of educational researchers to embrace this genre of study hinges on skepticism regarding the rigor and empirical nature of autoethnographic research. Even still, the breadth of this methodology's contribution to the field enlarges sociocultural critiques of education, calls attention to transparency of the researchers' methods, as well as their positionality, thereby not only challenging traditional ways of doing and representing research, but also providing new insights into a variety of educational issues (Alexander, 2006b; Delamont, 2007; Hughes, 2008; Pennington, 2007). Despite its increased usage among educational researchers, autoethnography is still met with a level of resistance within the field.

In *Public Education and the Imagination-Intellect* (2003), Mary Weems deploys poetry, playwriting, narrative, and paintings to devise an autoethnographic text that illumines the relationship between education, imagination, and social inequity. Through a dialogue between present-day realities of education and her imagination, Weems creates an invocation for imagination-intellect, an educational intervention and frame for cultivating a utopian-esque space of learning. The creative is grounded in people of color, resistance, and worldmaking. With a long history of women-of-color cultural workers ascribed and described as feminists, womanist, mothers, artists, and healers, the creative feeds cultural and social change. "The need to call attention to creativity as a mode of knowledge production genuinely engaged in and perfected by many women of color feminists-artists-scholars is also a call to create and encourage creativity" (Brown, 2013, p. 12). In *Who Look at Me?!: Shifting the Gaze of Education through Blackness, Queerness, and the Body*, we use performance to utilize the creative and implore read(er)s to consider how to better see Black people and youth. Specifically, what shifts must be made – individually, culturally, socially, collectively – to see the lived experiences of Black and Blackqueer people as both sites of knowledge and educational intervention?

A NOTE TO OUR READ(ER)S

Articulated in the prologue, the act of reading is a cultural, social, and political act with grave consequences for those things and people being read. Rooted in Black, queer cultural practices of being read and reading, to be a read(er) of this text explicitly places Blackness, queerness, education, and the read(er)s' historical relationship to and assumptions about these sites of being at the forefront. Furthermore, we envision read(er)s to be, though not exclusively, education stakeholders and people interested in seeing Blackness and queerness through a lens of possibilities. Operating from the conception that education is a lifelong process that happens in and beyond schools and shapes and is shaped by sociocultural realities, education stakeholders here refers specifically to researchers interested in and curious about Black youth lived experiences and individuals committed to learning and/or deepening personal and cultural awareness reflexivity practices, especially teachers, educators, and cultural workers.

ORGANIZATION OF THE BOOK

This book works through several different gazes, attending to sociological scripts and the interplay of cultural articulations of iconicity, (mis) recognition, culture, politics, and power as they play out within our social world. Moving between, within, and against these various gazes, we map out an understanding of gaze in relationship to particular communities (e.g., Black youth), contexts (e.g., within schools), and scale (e.g., micro/ individual, mezzo/community, macro/society). Each chapter asks three fundamental questions, reverberating Jordan (1969): who looks, who sees, and when looking, what is seen? Recognizing that what is seen depends on who is viewing, we reflect on the gazes cast on our particular bodies, in particular spaces, and how we have worked against, within, and in support of these gazes (Fleetwood, 2011). Further, each chapter insists that these questions require epistemological, methodological, and theoretical responses and shifts by providing various interventions in relationship to each.

Taking cues from the sutured fields enmeshed in our study of Blackness, queerness, education, and the body, we offer here an insistence on creative pedagogies and qualitative research methodologies that might provide freedom, shifting the gaze and thus the deleterious effects created in how we view Black youth, educators, and communities. The labor of exploring Jordan's question, "Who look at me?" and insisting that this looking be intersectional, dimension-filled, and just, requires us to engender a journey that (i) takes us into and through bodies (our bodies) that have been looked at and misread, (ii) names alternative tools for seeing and painting perspective with more colors, (iii) provides examples of these tools in action, and (iv) affirms the process of interrogating what we see, the arsenals we utilize for seeing, and what these say about us, as a moment steeped in possibilities for healing and shifting. Utilizing performance, the body, and the creative force of the arts as central elements in our research, we simultaneously indict the visual fields of gaze that surveil the Black body while also offering it up as a site of possibility and redress.

Following this introduction, we share a myriad of representations illuminating the gaze imposed onto Blackness and queerness, interpret these gazes, and discuss how performance and auto/ethnography in particular might intervene. Holding in tandem the site and sight of Blackness, each chapter differently addresses, how, when, and where we see Blackness, the effects of misrecognition, and possible anecdotes to address and redress the violence. Overall, the book moves through examining the formal educational gaze and its impacts on the valuation of Black and queer bodies particularly as meted out by teacher-student dynamics, followed by the informal educational gaze-the social curriculum which manifests as a means of foreclosing networks of care towards Black and queer communities, turning that gaze on its head as it comes into contact with Blackqueer gazes which imagine Black and queer communities differently. Moving from these broad contexts, we shift to Black girl gazes, illuminating the ways that Black girls are seen to themselves and what we can learn differently when attuned to their gaze rather than sociological gazes that seek to lock Black bodies into carceral geographies. Lastly, we turn to methodological gazes, how do we bring together epistemological frameworks of seeing and knowing minoritized communities into conversation with the very ways we do research specifically as it relates to autoethnography. To provide further reflection upon the primary arguments and gazes attended to in the chapters, reflection questions are offered at the end of each, with activities and workshop references provided for some chapters.

Chapter 1, "When You See Me: Notes on Terrible Educations," is an invitation into the authors' bodies through the narration of their schooling experiences. Through poetry and fictionalized accounts, this chapter names and describes two particularly salient educators and documents how the authors' embodied experiences of miseducation shaped them. Equally important, it illumines unlearning as a pedagogy of resistance to miseducation and asks read(er)s to bear witness to and confront historic residue and personal involvement in perpetuating educational spaces that are antithetical to the success and survival of Black communities.

Chapter 2, "Reflections on *Bodies on Display*: Exploring the Radical Potential of the Black, Queer Body," is a multilayered excavation of the performance-based autoethnographic work of our collective, Hill L. Waters. First, it provides an excerpt from an original performance, *Bodies on Display: An Exploration of Love, Intimacy, Violence, & The Black, Queer Body*, written, directed, and performed by us, as an example of the many directions of gaze and the work of each. In accounting for the ways the Black and queer body is read and misread, we offer a performative illustration of the relationship between gaze and bodies. To create a new way of seeing each other, and accordingly, the Black and queer body, we posit pleasure as the lens through which read(er) s must see our Blackqueer bodies and place it in dialogue with the written performance script and pictures taken of us during our performance.

Continuing to consider the possibility imbued in collectivity, Chapter 3, "Looking Again: Collective Visions, Collective Sight/Seeing," moves away from particular levels of gaze to articulate and counter the reading/misreading of the particular affinity group with whom we advocate and work: Black girls. Extending lessons and Black feminist pedagogy learned in SOLHOT, this chapter illustrates the potential of Black feminist organizing approaches and the personal work necessary to work with youth in affirming and ethical ways. Specifically, we argue that reorienting must occur epistemically and methodologically to work with youth, particularly Black girls, in ways that locate the daily lived experiences of youth as sites of political mobilization and knowledge creation.

To center spirit and collectivity, Chapter 4, "Answering the Call: Centering Spirit in Auto/Ethnography," envisions auto/ethnography as a Black, queer collective and spiritual praxis. Originally performed at the 2016 International Congress of Qualitative Inquiry as part of the Autoethnography Special Interest Group, and later published in the *International Review of Qualitative Research Journal*, "Answering the Call" writes to imagine anew the life chances and life possibilities of Black, queer people. Additionally, it invites read(er)s to take seriously: Where are Black youth in auto/ethnography? What is education (as in K-12) missing by not taking a vested interest in auto/ ethnography? What would a conversation between the field of education, an auto/ethnographic informed performance, and a Black feminist ethos look like? This chapter argues that Black girl worldmaking and Black women's sensibilities refashion the "I" in autoethnography. Moreover, that these lenses provide education opportunities to locate Blackness beyond spectacle.

Critical of and committed to engaging academe on our terms, Chapter 5, "When We Look at Each Other: An Auto/ethnography of Togetherness," names and refuses standard academic politics, and augments love and collective praxis in its place. Shifting the gaze of academic success from external measures to internal and interpersonal ones, this chapter outlines the intentionality of our methodology and illustrates the usefulness of collectivity and autoethnography as tools for inciting social justice, as well as more just visions of raced, gendered, sexualized, and all currently *othered* bodies and identities in and beyond academe. To close, we offer three scenes of Blackness that stir, trouble, and highlight the importance of sociocultural realities and the primary lenses that map onto Blackness and Black possibility. Staging the convergence of the site of harm and potential, and the accompanying sights of misrecognition and celebration, each scene recounts personal experiences to provide additional insights into the costs and gains of our gazes. Reading culture as curriculum and pedagogic, we turn to pop culture and everyday culture as a means of re-visualizing Blackness, Black education, and how we are educated about Blackness. Inspired by Baldwin's (1998) usage of letter writing as a form of intergenerational knowledge creation and dialogue, we round out the book with a letter to Uncle Jimmy (the late James Baldwin) reflecting on his words as they relate to the current state of education.

REFLECTION QUESTIONS & INTERACTIVE EXERCISE

General Questions

- Reflect upon your current gaze. What are your first thoughts when thinking about Blackness and queerness?
- What are the ways in which you see Blackness and queerness in conversation within your professional and everyday worlds?

For Educators

- When thinking about those youth with whom you regularly engage, what qualities about their identities do you automatically notice?
- How does Blackness and queerness show up in your educational space?

Recognizing the Rub

Directions: Draw a Venn diagram and label the two outer circles *Blackness* and *queerness*. Record characteristics and things that come to mind about Blackness and then about queerness. After doing so, repeat the process for the overlapping space, writing characteristics and words that come to mind for Black queerness. Review your diagram. What do you notice about the descriptors in each? Record your reactions to your Venn diagram, the ways you see Blackness and queerness connecting, and any other observations you have.

NOTES

[1] The student's name has been changed to a pseudonym.

[2] A collective co-organized by Ruth Nicole Brown beginning in 2006, SOLHOT is an intergenerational space dedicated to elucidating and celebrating Black girls and Black girlhood. Ruth Nicole Brown's understanding that Black girls often vie for space, that Black girls would benefit from attention and space, and that Black girlhood is a powerful location to work from and organize around, prompted her insistence to manifest SOLHOT. In its many and interlaced iterations (i.e., after-school program, We Levitate girl band, performances, academic conferences, and publications), SOLHOT casts Black girls and women as vital storytellers, visionaries, and problem solvers. Through artistic and performative mediums, SOLHOT documents, narrates, and imagines Black girlhood and what it means to be a Black girl in the world.

[3] This question opened up the Q&A portion of Ruth Nicole Brown's University of Missouri Qualitative Research Consortium talk entitled, "Tiara: 'Endangered Black Girls' Instructions 301" in Spring 2012.

[4] There are multiple ways to do SOLHOT. For instance, analog SOLHOT is "where we meet physically face to face, heart to heart, and hand to hand, to discuss issues that are important to us" (SOLHOT). Analog SOLHOT is currently organized in Champaign-Urbana, Illinois with a group of girls, women, and those who love Black girls. Intentional SOLHOT is the practice of using your whole self, time, talents, and resources to the service and benefit of Black girls everywhere. There is also digital SOLHOT, which manifests through the band and practice of We Levitate, Black girlhood celebration through musical, sonic, and digital expressions. See solhot.weebly.com

1. WHEN YOU SEE ME

Notes on Terrible Educations

When Mrs. Stansberry sarcastically dismissed my dream of being the first Black president of the United States, and when Mr. Dodd repeatedly called my Black peers and I "so stupid," their deliberations on our worth were final. These two elementary school teachers, with some unknown and arbitrary formula, determined the extent of our life chances and possibilities. In quick, verbal body blows, they peeled away pieces of our innocence. Under their class roof, we came to know that our success, our dreams of who we could be, were perhaps limited and would require battle.

Utilizing imagery, poetry, and fictionalized accounts, we illuminate pivotal moments of terrible education. These instances serve as pathways into our assertions of what education should be and what schooling tells you education is, and invites read(er)s to consider the ramifications of Black bodies subjected to schooling and not education. While reading, we encourage you to reflect on the articulations included and consider: *What was seen? Who looked? How?*

***

TERRIBLE EDUCATIONS I: THE (MIS)EDUCATION OF A POET

Way down in the jungle deep, when Black folks knew how to fly and OJ was free and bobos were still in style and high-top fades were not on the comeback. Back before Baltimore became synonymous with the melodramatic HBO series The Wire, a half-baked depiction of my city. Back before No Child Left Behind became an empty promise for generations of Black genius that standardized tests have yet to latch on to. Back when I believed without question that Black folks could be anything they wanted to be. When "why not" was not a possibility, "how" was not important, and "when" was simply a matter of time.

Back then, I wanted to be the first African-American president of these United States of America. The year was 1992, the same year "Barry" Barack Obama solidified his "Can Do No Wrong" card. A Black man

© KONINKLIJKE BRILL NV, LEIDEN, 2019 | DOI:10.1163/9789004392243_002

fresh out of Harvard Law, marrying the one and only Michelle LaVaughn Robinson, who would be the only reason I halfway trusted her too-smooth-talkin-sellin-us-hope-and-responsibility-freedom-preachin-drone-droppin-only-reflection-I-got-in-44-elected husband.

Me and my round, pound cake colored self (you know, the inside part) had moved through all the P's possible before settling on president. First was a police officer, then I wanted to be a politician, and for a brief moment as if foreseeing my own future, I wanted to be a preacher. Pilot did not make the cut at all, neither did parole officer, nor pharmacist or paramedic. My momma was a paramedic at the time, but I wanted to be THE FIRST African-American president.

But pound cake colored boys, you know like on the inside, who come from my side of the tracks cannot be the president of much else except prisons. That is what Mrs. Stansberry told me, in front of the whole class. So she says, through bright purple lipstick, "Hmph, what do you want to be when you grow up?"

Sharply, without missing a beat, I said, "The first Black president."

"Hmph, the first Black president? Silly as you are, you won't be much else than the president of somebody's penitentiary." Silence falls. The dialogue ended. Point one for the infamously dreaded substitute teacher with frizzled orange hair, slightly balding in the middle, on brownie-colored skin. Mrs. Stansberry strikes again!

It is now way after watching Mandela become elected President of South Africa; just some time after I realized RuPaul really was not a woman, meaning that my mama had been right all along, as mamas tend to be; just a little after Black women's love came and found me, for who knows what umpteenth time this is; sometime after we lost MJ to some weird combination of fame, vitiligo, and being Black in America; and after we realized Whitney had been drowning all along, and that there are just some things an autopsy will never tell us.

It is after kids no longer play outside, after metal detectors are in every school on the South Side of Chicago, yet Sandy Hook still rocks parts of our nation. Yes, even after the Million Man March, all of the 50-year commemorations of the Civil Rights Movement, and just after Don't Ask, Don't Tell is repealed, marriage equality is gaining traction, and school choice is the only choice. It is well after selfies are a thing,

Twitter beefs are real, after Blue Ivy is almost trademarked, and after we ask Black girl gold medalist Olympians to not only win gold but look good while doing it.

It is well after we know the price of silence in Rwanda. And I want to go back to the silence, back to Hilton Elementary. Back to the day that my round, pound cake colored self, you know like on the inside, squared off with Mrs. Stansberry and lost. Back to the moment I had gotten in trouble one too many times for the same thing that has gotten most Black boys and girls in trouble: our mouths. Either talking too much, not at the right time, not talking enough, caught whistling at white girls, quenching thirst with Arizona tea, daring to kiss girls and like it, asking the wrong questions on Fruitvale platforms on New Year's Eve. Black mouths, whether open or shut, do not seem to have access to the Obama "Can Do No Wrong" card.

I would like to go back and say something like, "Well you know what? My grandmother, and my mother, and my uncle, and Sistah Mabel, and Rev'ren Bailey, and Mama and Papa Isabelle, and Sistah Louise, and Sistah Shirley, and Miss Marva alllllllll seem to think I could be. They keep tellin' me I can be anything I wanna be when I grow up." Score one for the pound cake colored boy, you know like on the inside. The class is hysterical. There are oooohs and ahhhhs and he's gonna get it and giggles. Nobody liked Mrs. Stansberry, and I mean noooooobody (Callier, 2016a).

Mrs. Stansberry was my (mis)education. Before graduate school, where I learned words like "culturally responsive pedagogy" and "critical theory," I was intimately familiar with the concept of "terrible educations" (Bambara, 1996, p. 255). In spite of Mrs. Stansberry and the multiple iterations of her in society as disciplinary limits, conservative education research methodologies, and an overemphasis on schooling versus learning, I learned that education was expansive. Because of my community, I learned education should be emancipatory, culturally relevant, artistic, kinesthetic, accessible, and communal (Bambara, 1996). Learning and education should not be measured and equated with traditional schooling processes. It is time that we have research methods and questions that reflect the reality that education takes place beyond schools.

***

TERRIBLE EDUCATIONS II: "WHEN IT GETS IN THE BLOOD"

He entered me/

Red-toupee-wearing Mr. Dodd/Entered me/

Fix me/

Tried to/

Be a lady – Why are you sitting like that?

Why you being so Black/So stupid/

He entered me/

Stabbed my thighs closed/

Felt like/Thought I heard/Don't be so Black/

Come here, I'll fix you/

Without my permission/He entered/

Exited/

Entered, This time a woman/

No old white man/

Women who raised me/

Fix me/

Tried to/

Be more ladylike

Books on my head/

My posture fixed, temporarily/

She, they entered me/

Exited/

Entered/

Teacher/

Another, another, then another

Fix me/Tried/Well-meaning/

Good intentions/Fix me/

More like break me/My spirit/

Without permission/Enter me/

Try to/Fix me/

Success!/It's in my skin/

I cry/Fix, you try/

Broken, I am/

It's in my skin/

Without permission, entered/

Exited/Entered/They did/

But it never left/

(Hill, 2013)

REFLECTIONS

Short-circuit-tempered Mr. Dodd. With little patience for his active, curious, and not about to just accept anything students, he found every opportunity to snap and insult. At least it felt that way. On countless occasions, he insisted that his previous teaching experience at a different school, a school known to be more white and more selective, was better. That we were "stupid" and just didn't care. He made fun of how I and others sat in our seats, insisted that the girls sit up straight with our legs closed.

Mr. Dodd, my fifth-grade teacher, taught me domestication. Mr. Dodd instructed me on the rules of engagement regarding being successful in school. He pointed out/at improper moves I made during my pursuit of fifth-grade success. But Mr. Dodd, my short, white, toupee-wearing fifth-grade teacher, who was quick to yell epithets that indicated a lack of respect for and little belief in our ability to achieve academically, did not disappear upon my move to sixth grade. Instead, he haunted me until my mid-20s; I came to see Mr. Dodd as a verb, an evolving and chameleon-like character vessel serving up training lessons on how to practice domestication. To "Mr. Dodd" is to implement policies and inflict harm, explicit or implicit, that create restraints and confine imagined life chances and possibilities resembling sociocultural structures and realities.

NAMING & UNLEARNING: PEDAGOGIES OF RESISTANCE

Of course we know how to walk on the water, of course we know how to fly; fear of sinking, though, sometimes keeps us from the first crucial move, then too, the terrible educations you liable to get is designed to make you destruct the journey entire. (Bambara, 1996, p. 255)

Terrible education is dangerous. It teaches us, trains us even, to act against our self-interest, against actualizing our gifts. Bambara (1996) articulates the interlaced realities of fear, action, and miseducation. Building on this work, we take up how the care experienced by students from marginalized backgrounds, both inside and outside of school settings, is indicative of a cultural education, or what M. Jacqui Alexander (2005) notes as pedagogies, "...both epistemic and ontological project bound to our beingness" (p. 7). Who we be, when we look at each other? Further, as Alexander (2005) moves us to note in *Pedagogies of Crossing*, knowledge is created and passed down in ritual. We learn – who we should be, how others see us, and therefore how we should be treated – in relationship. Thus, what do we make of the quotidian and ritualized practices of terrible educations (i.e., abuse of the Black, queer body, appraisals of inferiority, poverty, culturally deviant)? Each of these cultural treatments of the Black body denote a form of terrible education, pedagogies which instruct us of the value of Black youth, educators, and persons, and how in kind we should deal with Black communities and one another. This is, as Alexander (2005) illuminates, "the fundamentally pedagogic imperative at its heart: the imperative of making the world in which we live intelligible to ourselves and to each other – in other words, teaching ourselves" (p. 6). Or stated differently, how might we see one another more fully when we affix our gazes, personal, political, cultural, and spiritual, onto one another?

In the preceding cases, Mrs. Stansberry and Mr. Dodd facilitated miseducation processes by insisting that our self-concepts were inaccurate. More specifically, each assessed our life chances and life possibilities to be less expansive than those we saw for ourselves. In her autobiography, Assata Shakur (2001) makes claims about the reason behind low teacher expectations asserting, "Schools in amerika are interested in brainwashing people with amerikanism, giving them a little bit of education, and training them in skills needed to fill the positions the capitalist system requires" (p. 181). In other words, schools are not designed to actually educate students. They are instead conceptualized as spaces for ensuring the strength of the United States economy, of which consciousness, social justice, and equity are immaterial. Said differently, in *Too Much Schooling, Not Enough Education*, Shujaa (1998) asserts, "Schooling is a process intended to perpetuate and maintain the society's existing power relations and the institutional structures that support these arrangements" (p. 15). This conception of schooling supports Shakur's statement and denotes a difference between schooling and education. Applying this frame as analytic affords a deeper understanding of Mr. Dodd's and Mrs. Stansberry's negligence and practice of terrible educations. Specifically, their limited assessments of who each of us could be aligns with their complicity in status quo practices and power structures. When gazing upon our bodies, they at best could not and at worst refused to see us beyond the social scripts given to them about Black urban youth. These social scripts administered through media, popular culture, research, and institutional practices often negatively characterized and limited the life chances and life possibilities of Black urban youth through reading their attitudinal dispositions (e.g., acting white, sass, refusing to assimilate, etc.), socioeconomic backgrounds, familial makeup, and cultural capital as deficits (Fordham & Ogbu, 1986; Moyihan, 1965; Owens, Ford, Lisbon, Jones, & Owens, 2016; Smith & Harper, 2015).

But why? How could *these* teachers comfortably think so little of us, of our dreams? We cannot consult them and attain the answers to these questions. We can, however, consider how their perceptions connect to, echo, and even reproduce social attitudes and structures that shape the enterprise of education. Additionally, we can take direction from scholarship exploring the educational experiences of students pushed to the margins. Examining the road toward academic success, research illustrates that students from traditionally marginalized groups experience extensive personal and community costs (Jones, 2010; Lim, 2008; Rollock, 2007). An example of this is a literacy program in which McArthur and Muhammed (2017) explored the sociocultural realities shaping the lives of African-American Muslim girls. In particular, this four-week program comprised the girls writing letters to future generations of African-American Muslim girls. In these letters, the girls speak truths about discrimination and the complexities of being African-American Muslim girls, and offer advice for navigating the socio-cultural terrain. Equally pertinent is the information embedded within these letters – how society sees/disappears African-American Muslim girls.

When assessing the potential success of Black girls, emphasis is frequently placed on their particular performances of femininity (Campbell, 2012;

27

Fordham, 1993; Horvat & Antonio, 1999; Lei, 2003; Morris, 2007; Stitzlein, 2008). Similarly, concerning the gaze upon Black boys' experiences in attaining success in navigating institutional and community spaces, normative performances of white-male, heteronormative masculinities are either the primary subject of analysis or highlighted as a preferred attribute and pathway toward success (McCready, 2010a; McCready, 2010b; Warren, 2014). This misrecognition, as McCready (2010b) suggests, creates a missed opportunity for Black males and Black, queer males in particular, given that their performances of (Black) masculinity and sexuality disrupt beliefs and norms which assume Black men to be hyper-masculine, heterosexual thugs. Further, as Prudence Carter (2005) suggests, our notions of Black youth's disavowal of whiteness often misses the mark in terms of how we understand Black youth's desires, self-ascribed forms of success, and ability to navigate school and society in ways that draw upon multiple forms of social and cultural capital. More to the point, Carter (2005), McCready (2010a, 2010b), and Warren (2014) demonstrate that when we look at Black youth and Black male youth with whitewashed lenses, our perception of the issues they face often miss the impact of intersecting forms of systemic oppression which impend on their progress and success.

The amalgam of race and sexuality as entangled matrices of domination (Collins, 1990) escalate and layer the gaze and its impact in educational spaces. For instance, as Callier (2016b) argues, regarding queer-of-color youth experiences,

> The monocausal framing of the issues as illustrated by popular responses to Sakia, Jaheem, and Carl miss the systemic ways that race, sexuality, class, youthfulness, and gender (expression) simultaneously structure the lives of youth. Such frames ignore how issues of race, ethnicity, and class interact with issues of homophobia and antiqueer antagonisms. (p. 3)

Further, such frames, in their lack of intersectional analysis, still leave marginalized students, such as Black and queer youth, to experience violence both within and outside of schools (Blackburn, 2007; Callier, 2016; McCready, 2004; Pritchard, 2013).

Taken together, youth from marginalized backgrounds, particularly Black youth, inclusive of Black girls and Black, queer youth, experience gazes which inherently see them and their cultures as wrong (Dickar, 2008; Grant, 1994; Henry, 1998; Lei, 2003; Morris, 2007; Watkins, Lewis, & Chou, 2001), deficient, and in need of correction. Moreover, this sort of educational gaze predicated upon difference as deficient, primarily foregrounds a looking at a distant observation of object-making, rather than looking with a subject-making relationality of beingness to beingness (Fanon, Sartre, & Farrington, 1963; Wynter & McKittrick, 2015). For instance, in several of these studies on Black girls, researchers' perspectives and readings of the girls are centered (Neal-Jackson, 2018). The girls are not consulted, which denotes a preoccupation with the girls' ability to meet standards of legibility that align with normative social and cultural standards. Black girls are being subjected to a gaze onto their experiences that remains voyeuristic, presumptuous, and power-laden.

Similarly, Prier (2012) documents problems associated with gaze as it pertains to Black boys in urban education. Along with the voices of the young participants in his research, Prier attests to the politics and power of hegemony and its participation in (mis)reading Black boys in educational spaces. In particular, he articulates the subversive and vital cultural alignment that emanates from students' deployment of a hip-hop aesthetic through speech, dress/clothing, and performance. These same enactments, however, in the eyes of many (non-Black, non-youthful) stakeholders, serve as symbols of criminality and delinquency. What we have highlighted here are the ways gaze manifests upon the appraisal of Black skin, and the resulting consequences (e.g., loss of hair,[1] life,[2] and educational opportunities). In the chapters that follow, we offer exemplars of pedagogy and practices that create generative and productive ways of examining Black girls and boys, ways that afford more weight to how they make meaning of their realities, ways of seeing and being seen as Black, whole, and human. Furthermore, in exploring the optics of the gaze, we illustrate that *who* is looking matters just as much as *how,* and explore what can be done to shift our relations of sight.

I AM, WE ARE, BEFORE THAT: LETTERS TO THE FUTURE[3]

By elucidating terrible educations, we point to both the historical and contemporary issues within education that shape the gaze in which we view, and subsequently, how we treat Black youth. Rooted in our own life histories, we have felt deeply the effects of this gaze. Moreover, we know now that the gaze persists in similar yet distinct ways from our fateful encounters with Mrs. Stansberry and Mr. Dodd. Despite this, we close this chapter with an open letter to our niece and nephew. Joining a Black epistolary tradition, political, spiritual, and familial, we write to our loved ones with their futures in mind. Reflecting on our own pasts, we also articulate an insistence, as Black feminist troublemaker Alexis Pauline Gumbs (2016) penned, "i am before that…before black is bad and broken i am more. i am not coin or token. i am deepest spell spoken. and you are shook" (p. 131). This is our hope, knowing that a future generation, our beloveds, might also know.

Dear Ayanna and Cobi,

We write to you with a sense of urgency because we do not know what the future holds for us. What we know is our hope for the both of you. And what we also know is that this country owes you, like it owes every "son and daughter," but especially you, Black girl and Black boy child. A madman and his cronies now sit in the seat of power, governing our country toward the destruction of every public good, which many of us so desperately need. An unqualified lot in both moral aptitude and expertise, the swindlers have made our lives and your lives much harder. So we write to share with you the auspiciousness of this moment.

"To be young, gifted, and black is where it's at." That's what Nina said, or perhaps said differently by Kendrick, "we gon' be alright." Family, friends, teachers, and haters may try to convince you otherwise. Society will likely create images and narratives that present false, mythic, and/ or unreliable depictions of you. This was certainly true in our lives and the lives of those before us.

We have had the fortunate experience of being seen for who we are and who we might be able to be: infinite. For Uncle Rell, being seen by Mrs. Stewart (now Ms. Pinnick) and Ms. Burwell at Hilton Elementary School mattered just as much then as it does now. The gift of sight they gave to me, a vision of unbridled opportunity and endless possibilities, is the same gift we want to give to both of you. Your Auntie Dom had some interesting run-ins with teachers because they took issue with my mouth. In that regard, Mrs. Metzger, my fourth-grade teacher, was no different. Simultaneously though, she encouraged me to write about my feelings and be a class leader. When class got too live for her or we needed to travel to another part of the building, she called on me to set an example. Perhaps she paid too much attention to me, but I knew she saw me as more than "having a mouth on her," as old Black folks might say. This too is our hope, that you will receive over and over again the gift of being seen and seeing yourself clearly.

Cobi, in case you were waiting for someone to tell you, you are okay, handsome, and capable of anything. I am here to tell you, you are capable of being more than I could dream for you. Know that you are okay, handsome, and your possibilities are endless. I watch you draw, pick up your Auntie NaeNae's guitar, and create images made of chords and shapes seen first in your mind. Cobi, those are sightings of genius. The world, and possibly some older loved ones, will call it scribble and noise. Don't believe us/them. Trust what makes you smile and keep doing those things. On a summer visit in Bmore, you mentioned having fashion in your future. If that passion remains, count me in for contributing to your education in that area. If that changes, know that's okay too. Always remember, it's okay to change. Better yet, it's expected. Cobi, I need you to know your power so that no one, not even family, can make you feel less than. This world swallows children up, especially Black children. You have too many undiscovered and brewing talents and too much light to be devoured. Cobi, always hold on to what feels good to you.

I see you, Ayanna, bright bold brilliant blazing star. You are not your mother's fears nor this society's erratic anxieties – what more can the delusion of racial hierarchy and capitalist consumption to our own detriment be? They would have you think that you are wrong in all your genius and marvel. That the Mississippi mud hue of you, mixed with "good" (Black) hair, those tangles of geometric architecture, galaxies even, they would have you believe those things are nothing. But you are everything. Black. Is. Everything. Try not to wait too long to know this. Hold on to it when they try to show you your reflection in illusion mirrors. Know that we, Yaya, Gran, Nang, and her mother's mother's mother said it first. You are a force of our wildest dreams, manifesting futures better than our present in the small simple act of seeing yourself clearly and loving that self endlessly. Black girl child, our first (and yes, still my favorite) niece, you are the baddest and blessed, above and not beneath, more than enough, the universe perfected on the edge of bursting galaxies of endless laughter, Black joy, and Black girl genius. Do you see it? I do.

This letter is to your brilliance, your potential, and your alrightness. Always hold close the truth about who you are, and to Ayanna & Cobi, let no one determine that 'cept you.

Love,

Auntie Dom & Uncle Rell

REFLECTION QUESTIONS

General Questions

- Which terrible education story, Mrs. Stansberry or Mr. Dodd, did you relate most to and why?
- How does gaze shape educational experience?

For Educators

- According to Hill & Waters, what made each education terrible?
- How do you connect with and/or disengage from the two notes on terrible educations?
- Based on these stories, what are you taking away about gaze and being an educator?
- How do you resist your internally learned or systemically driven Mr. Dodd and Mrs. Stansberry in your teaching and pedagogy?

NOTES

[1] In December 2009, seven-year-old Lamya Cammon was asked to the front of the classroom by her teacher and sent back to her desk crying, missing one braid that her teacher cut off with a pair of classroom scissors.

[2] Carl Joseph Walker Hoover was an eleven-year-old Black boy who committed suicide after persistent homophobic violence and anti-gay slurs (Simon, 2009).

[3] See Gumbs (2016), "i am before that [...] before black is bad and broken i am more" (p. 131).

2. REFLECTIONS ON BODIES ON DISPLAY

Exploring the Radical Potential of the Black, Queer Body

In part we grew
by looking back at you […]

black face black body and black mind
beyond obliterating. (Jordan, 1969, p. 66)

We were (still are) angry. And, like Lorde (1984), we wanted to put our anger to productive use. We were (still are) thinking with all of our being. And, like other Black, queer, feminist, and liminally located insurgents, we felt compelled to create. Angry, deeply reflecting, and moved to fashion new ways to see ourselves somewhere between mournful and still alive, reverent yet hopeful, we created *Bodies on Display: An Exploration of Love, Intimacy, Violence, and the Black, Queer Body.* As culmination of a performance ethnography project, *Bodies on Display* illuminates Blackness, queerness, and violence as entangled webs of context and meaning.

Organized around three themes – pain, pleasure, and possibility – it offers synthesis, critique, and coalescence of larger discourses of anti-Black and anti-queer sentiment, as well as their mappings onto our quotidian experiences. As filters through which Black, queer bodies are seen and sites that help make and disassemble Blackness, queerness, and Blackqueerness, they build upon, talk back to, and reinforce each other. For the purpose of this chapter, however, we focus specifically on pleasure. To disorient and work from anarrangement (Moten, 2003), we center pleasure as a pathway for creating Blackqueer alterity. Our intentional choice here is rooted in a demand that Blackqueer pleasure be seen for three primary reasons. First, it brings visibility to pleasure, an often invisible or presumed unavailable resource to be accessed by Blackness, especially in the current milieu plagued by Black death, police violence, and Black youth disappearing. Second, it forces viewers to reckon with Black bodies doing things and being themselves in ways that denote sovereignty (Dillard, 2016), self-definition, and joy. Third, it intentionally narrows the frame of gaze to examine Black, queer bodies' relationship(s) to pleasure and what constitutes pleasure for these bodies and individuals.

© KONINKLIJKE BRILL NV, LEIDEN, 2019 | DOI:10.1163/9789004392243_003

To accomplish this task, this chapter places the performance, *Bodies on Display* (*BoD*) in conversation with pictures taken during its full showing on March 9, 2016 at the University of Alabama as part of the Discerning Diverse Voices Symposium, as well as recent theorization of the show and the visual archive from this showing generated from Jonathan Norris, the photographer. Emulating a scrapbook, this chapter provides a snippet of the performance/script, reflections around the show debut and the new archive – photographs, reflective memories, ephemera – created from our bodies being on display to interrogate the following: What happens when a body is on display? When it's a Black body, does the queerness illuminate? How do the answers to these questions connect to gaze? Who is looking at the body, and where?

Set as a live-art installation vis-à-vis a living mobile museum, this performance employs our bodies – through self-authored poetry, movement, and a series of visual images – to explore the interwoven relationships of race, gender, and sexuality, and render the Blackqueer body visible. Using our own life stories, as well as an amassed archive of newspaper clippings, news reports, and personal journal entries and reflections, we created poetry to synthesize and make sense of the archive informing our show and the questions we were seeking to explore through performance. The original poetry draws on biographically true moments and reflections to consider the pain, pleasure, and possibilities experienced by Black and queer bodies. In doing so, we reveal the cultural curriculum that circulates about how Black and queer bodies can and should experience in the world, while also providing ways that the Blackqueer body imagines itself beyond such scripts.

More specifically, the performance takes up the Blackqueer body as both the seen and scene, as referenced by Harvey Young (2010). The Black body is seen – the "epidermalization of blackness the inscription of meaning onto skin color" (p. 1), and stages a scene – the spectacular event created when discursive imaginings of Blackness creates (deleterious) material realities (Young, 2010). In doing so, *Bodies on Display* engages the current cultural and political unrest centering around issues of how and which Black lives matter, take on value, and hold meaning. As an ideological and political intervention, the hashtag #BlackLivesMatter was devised and mobilized by Black, queer women as a national and international contestation of the various forms of injustice that negatively impact all Black people. Moreover, it served as an intersectional call to resist the multiple systems of oppression that often drive a wedge between Black and queer people.

The thrust of this chapter reflects on ways of seeing the Black, queer body through performance, and specifically by reflecting on our own performance work and practice. Overall, the performance highlights alternative entryways into the narratives of marginalized individuals/communities, while creating pathways to enact justice (Brown, 2013; Carlson, 1996; Denzin, 2003; hooks, 1990; Leavy, 2010; Madison & Hamera, 2006; Spry, 2011). To place our bodies on display is a practice intended to invite and employ witnesses to see the subject of interest (i.e., Black, queer bodies) and to trouble, disrupt, and confront, along with us, understandings of the intersections of art, justice, love, violence, Blackness, and queerness.

Furthermore, *Bodies on Display* highlights the value of Arts Based Research (ABR) to facilitate rethinking and re-imagining of student/teacher relationships, classroom culture, and the role of love and justice in educational research. Furthering the work of educational philosopher Maxine Greene (1995), cultural critics and educators like Elliot Eisner (2003, 2006, 2009), Paulo Freire (1970, 1973), bell hooks (1995a), Virginia Lea and Erma Jean Sims (2008), and scholar/artists Ruth Nicole Brown (2013), Augosto Boal (1985), June Jordan (1985, 1995), and Mary E. Weems (2003), this project demonstrates the rich and interwoven relationship between art, education, and social justice.

Through performance, we utilize the juxtaposition of our lived experiences with our intention to embody a complicated enactment upon the stage to demonstrate how our bodies act as interventions and sites of alternative visions. Moreover, we assert that by rendering visible the interlocking nature of Blackness, queerness, love, and violence, a more complex portrait of Black livelihood is brought into view.

Reflecting on the performance, this chapter begins with providing an articulation of the body and offers a performative text comprising illustrations, an excerpt from the *BoD* script, and our current reflections on these as a bodily archive of our bodies on display. Lastly, we close with "Notes on Pleasure and Blended Scripting: Reorienting the Gaze," a section that highlights the utility of pleasure in our performance, the methodological innovation in our text, the inspiration of Blended Scripting, and the multiple layers taken up to consider methodological ways of shifting the gaze.

DIMENSIONS OF BODY

For the purpose of understanding this chapter, as well as our larger collective practice, we assert that the body is subject and object, visceral and cerebral, producer and consumer of knowledge, part of an individual and collective body. It is therefore physical and more. These layers are particularly important when considering what is showcased of a body versus what is seen as body. In *BoD*, we offer a layered contextualization of the body with a focus on a collective Black and queer body, a body that individual Black and/or queer bodies are juxtaposed against. In recognition of the marking and appraisal of Black bodies as a political project (Hill, 2018), we subvert the auction block metaphor of how Black bodies are typically seen—abject, defunct, and pain-filled—by daring stand to be seen beyond the limited field of vision afforded Black and queer bodies. Harvey Young (2010) declares, "When popular connotations of blackness are mapped across or internalized within black people, the result is the creation of *the black body*. This second body, an abstracted and imagined figure, shadows or doubles the real one" (p. 7). The abstracted body then becomes part of popular social memory (Young, 2006, 2010). Accordingly, *BoD* recognizes this abstracted body and employs it as one layer of understanding Black bodies and gaze.

These popular and abstract images that have come to represent *the* Black body, despite their widespread acceptance and replication within society, continue to be contested, critiqued, and imagined by the everyday, individual lived experiences of being Black, as well as by scholars, cultural workers, and Black feminists. Related, feminist Jacquelyn Zita (1998) frames the body as "a materialization, a socially mediated formation, lived individually and in communities as *real effects*" (p. 4). This conceptualization brings into view the body as dynamic and contextually located, both an individual and collective entity, and posits the dialogic relationship between gaze and bodies. Often situated as a site not for our own pleasure, the Black body, our bodies are not available to ourselves for our own pleasures. Rather, the Black body is often the scene of someone else's enjoyment, a receptacle for someone else's pain, and a scene of someone else's imagined future and possibilities. Cognizant of this reality and appraisal of the Black body, *BoD* takes up the ways Black bodies are, are not, and could be seen. What we offer below is our intentional staging of Black pleasures. More importantly, these pleasures are located within Black sensibilities, for us, on our own terms. In doing so, the scenes reflect pleasure within and beyond the sexual to consider pleasure as joy and deep connection (hooks, 1994; Lorde, 1984), memory work and elegy (Pritchard, 2016), Black sovereignty (Dillard, 2016), endarkened feminist epistemology (Dillard & Okpalaoka, 2011), body-centered/performer-centered aesthetic/intervention (Jones, 1997), and feminist aesthetic/intervention (Bell, 1995). The artistic mediums utilized within the performance and presented below endeavor to illumine historic and contemporary moments of anti-Black violence and anti-queer violence and their imprints on our Black queer bodies. By deploying arts-based modes of inquiry to offer up our literal bodies and narratives, our bodies serve as interpolators to the oft mono-causal framing which ignores the intersections of Blackness and queerness.

Our decision to re-present the portion of the performance on pleasure is intentional. Considering the historical and discursive gazes upon Black bodies, we deliberately chose pleasure as the content of the Black bodies in view, the subject. We thought it of critical importance when writing this chapter that read(er)s engage with the less visible topic of pleasure. Disinterested in offering additional time and space to recurrent tropes, pathology, and other narratives that mark Blackness as something to be fixed and out of reach for those bodies and people who inhabit it, we endeavor for read(er)s, on our terms, to see Black, queer pleasure.

In the next section, we provide a performative illustration of the relationship between gaze and bodies. Specifically, we place pleasure in conversation with pictures taken of us during our debut performance of *Bodies on Display*, March 9, 2016 at the University of Alabama as part of the Discerning Diverse Voices Symposium. While perusing our bodies, please note the following: the pictures represent the physical body seen that day and captured at the will of the photographer. On the other hand, the script excerpt is an offering of knowledge production, including what the body knows as a result of being in a particular body, and discursive realities of our particular Black, queer bodies rubbing against the abstract Black body. Our decision within this chapter to juxtapose text and photographs to create a new way of seeing and understanding the script excerpt is two-fold: (i) to offer a reflexive and refractive gaze back onto the outward surveillance of our bodies, and (ii) to create a visual narrative accompaniment to reorient the gaze. The pictures and the corresponding text are not meant to mirror the actual performance. In that sense, what you see may or may not correspond to the actual gesture or embodied movements created when delivering lines. At other times, the associated picture is a corresponding and precise artifact of what was displayed during the performance. Our intention here is not to recreate the performance, and as performance scholars note, reflections of performance are in and of themselves performances (Jones, 2002). However, our intention here is to provide a space to reorient the outward gaze. Here, we are looking back at you, looking back at ourselves. We are seeing ourselves anew, inside pleasure, turning the gaze and the acknowledged associative pains into our own pleasures.

BODIES ON DISPLAY: PLEASURE[1]

DOCENT VI:[2]

Cue: Truth: "Our Land"[3]
HILL enters stage
Fade down "Our Land" at 1:43

HILL: We are entering another p. Whose p, I mean, what p are we entering? Anyone? Yes, we are entering pleasure, my second favorite p. What pleasures do you think are going to show themselves in this exhibit? Don't be shy. (Wait for ad libs.) These are all quite possible, but I'll let you experience this p all by yourself, kinda sorta. (smirks) The first piece of this portion is by artist...

Artist: Hill L. Waters

Medium: pleasure, memory, happy feelings, Black girl genius

Music Production: RyNeaSoul/WeLevitate/BlackGirlGeniusWeek

Title: "Don't It Feel Good?!"

Description: "Don't It Feel Good?!" is a poetic, performative analysis of Hill L. Water's interpretation of Black Girl Genius Week (or BGGW). Dreamed up and manifested by Ruth Nicole Brown and SOLHOT homegirls/boy,[4] BGGW was a week-long conjuration in November 2014 at the University of Illinois. "Don't It Feel Good?!" is an offering of what BGGW comprised and made happen, as well as the emotion, effect, and potential it incited.

Don't It Feel Good?!

Cue: We Levitate: "Black Girl Genius"
HILL and WATERS enter…sitting on the porch. WATERS playing in
HILL hair and greasing scalp <bring grease and comb>

WATERS: Just got my skateboard
and forged license to glide on the rainbow
who told us we couldn't fly?

HILL: found freedom
in a basement
black bass reverberating
Happy Feelings

HILL: Moons falling from my mouth
Heaven shining from beneath her fitted

WATERS: Watching him blossom
stretching his words, his mouth

BOTH: before the mic

WATERS: Brand new panties
without the crotch
bottomless,
Cuz Annie don't wear *no* panties (*sing-song*)

HILL: surfboard (as if singing "Drunk in Love")

WATERS: twerking from the pulpit of #Blackgirlgenius

Knowing and
SOLHOT became a
BOTH: we laid
HILL: touched
WATERS: and it
HILL: we were
BOTH: again
WATERS: brand
HILL: again
WATERS: whole
BOTH: again

remembering why, how, when
verb
hands on each other

was good
good

new

HILL: light breeze
BOTH: levitation

DOCENT VII

HILL: Well damn, sign me up. I'm packing a bag right now. If only our days were filled with loving kindness, no undergarments, and *surfboard.* Shall we keep digging out this p and letting it unravel? Shall we? (Wait for audience response.) Now this next piece is by an artist you should be getting familiar with…

Artist: Durell M. Callier
Medium: collage, paper, and re-memory on cardboard
Title: The American Dilemma

"The American Dilemma" is a collage that questions the relationship of the Black body to the American Dream. Unveiled through the curtains of the White House stands the lone figure of the Black child. An amputee standing upon a landmass, what does this child survey? What are his possibilities and which ones are foreclosed? What are the inheritances of the Black child, and how does pleasure pervade notions of American citizenship, meritocracy, and settler colonialism? When placing the Black child in relationship to the American imaginary, how does the Black child become cast as a queer figure? Or stated differently, how is the Black child within this context also a site of queerness? These issues are brought to bear in this collage.

American Dilemma[5]

WATERS enters stage holding a baby, works throughout scene to rock baby to sleep…

the night Mike
Brown was
indicted
i wanted to find
the sweetest
chocolate boy
hold him close
and whisper sweet

somethings in his ear
all night till

morning

tonight all the chocolate boys are hugging their chocolate babies a little closer
counting the blessings of breath
   heart beats
   and small sweet hands
watching tenderly
as they whisper

revolt

WATERS exits stage
WATERS returns to stage as EzB

DOCENT VIII

WATERS: "Know from whence you came. If you know whence you came, there are absolutely no limitations to where you can go." – James Baldwin
   Our next piece…
   Artist: Dominique C. Hill

Medium: poetry, desire

Title: "Transcendental Sex"

Description: "Transcendental Sex" works from desire and longing to create an imagined relationship unraveling between two women. Seeking to go beyond sex in the physical realm, "Transcendental Sex" engenders a journey into intimacy, a slow, mental penetration that takes the body on a ride, but emanates from the mental as well as from an interest in sustained pleasure.

Transcendental Sex

WATERS enters and takes his seat in school, seated at a desk or in a lecture chair…HILL enters as an instructor (bring whip)

HILL:
I. Make intense, deliberate, and inviting eye contact

II. Create a memorable introduction. Firmly rub Lucille, Harriet, Maya, Octavia, and Zora into my right palm

III. Smize and allure me into your words

IV. Lean in and offer up the truth about what color in my garb grabbed your attention and what about my name demands you hold off from quickly dropping your credentials

V. Name a warrior of the light whose legacy i know not

VI. Run circles around my left nipple with oral confessions of the goals you have and the dreams you have during the day with your eyes wide open

VII. To be continued…

DOCENT IX

WATERS: Got another gem for you…

"Now we think as we fuck this nut might kill. This kiss could turn to stone." – Essex Hemphill

Transcendental sex post the HIV epidemic being a gay man's disease

Post increasing infection rates of the virus among Black women

Post PrEP
Post Depo-Provera
Post post post post the orgasmicccccccc release…
Now we think…
This kiss could…

Still be pleasurable…

Moving on…
  Artist: Hill L. Waters
  Medium: spoken word, love, funk, sweat, sweetness
  Title: "Touch Me Here/Good Lovin"
  Description: "Touch Me Here/Good Lovin" explores the politics of pleasure and questions what it means to feel love, be love, and be loved. Locating the personal as political and the political as sacred work, "Touch Me Here" interrogates issues of longing and self-love, as well as intimacy with self and others.

Touch Me Here/Good Lovin
Cue: Good Lovin, Ludacris ft. Miguel

WATERS enters stage and approaches a door with flowers, knocks on door… HILL answers door. WATERS picks up HILL for a date, gives her a flower as they walk to the car

HILL:	WATERS:
when looking at myself after a shower	
reading sonia, lucille, audre, zora	touch me here and here
watching her long to be touched nipple biting first time, all of them	leave your mark right here
seeing myself with new eyes, hungry eyes seeing myself and feeling hungry what it feels like to know you taste good to see her, him, they, ze, pleased	essence of you mixed with my longing titillating i want to love and be loved by a Black man
her smile his twerk	love and be loved by love and be loved by I want to be
opening my legs and feeling a breeze on a hot summer's day cold water running down my back	right here legs intertwined
she pulls my hair	your head on my chest fluttering breaths
dancing to sleep	
waking to her laying in the arms of someone you know only through eye conversation	slight exhales fingers move charting this new ground
being able to BE and that be more than enough	unexpected sweet relief
feeling	stay
feeling	my head on your chest intertwined
	here

DOCENT X

HILL: Hunni p. parker is feeling and slightly purring right now. Hill L. Waters are a piece of work. Anyone know if Hill or Waters is single? Do you know? (Point to someone.) What do you think their story is? Like, are they an item? Were they ever? What is Waters into? You think Hill likes women who wear smiles? Or carry books and straps? (laughs) As usual, I digress. That's what happens when folk talk about desire and longing in front of me. Back to why you all are here. This next piece is sure to be a tasty treat as it also comes from artist:

Artist: Hill L. Waters

Medium: hope, stardust, red clay, inconvenient truths

Title: "The Challenge"

Description: "The Challenge" is a poem that lays the groundwork for the pivotal questions driving Hill L. Waters' work. It responds to the questions: What is the work? How do we make it pleasure-filled?

The Challenge

WATERS & HILL are on a corner/sitting, waiting to catch the bus…HILL is reading a newspaper. WATERS refuses to sit down next to HILL…

HILL: who are you loving

WATERS: how are you loving

HILL: that is the question

WATERS: who are you healing

HILL: how are you healing

WATERS: that is the work

HILL: loving

WATERS: healing

HILL: the work

Cue: Truth: "Our Land"

LEARNING THROUGH THE BODY: WHAT BEING
ON DISPLAY TAUGHT US

It is impossible to write the pleasurable embodiments we call performance
without tangling with the cultural stories, traditions, and political
contestations that comprise our sense of history. (Diamond, 1996, p. 1)

In opening this chapter, we offered an excerpt from June Jordan's (1969)
Who Look at Me, in which she says, "In part we grew/by looking back at
you [...] black face black body and black mind/beyond obliterating" (Jordan,
1969, p. 66). This declaration grounds our understanding of the possibility of
performances of Blackness that might restructure the gaze. Often, "racialized
heteronormativity structures the gaze and the field of vision," and while this is
true, Blackness exceeds such attachments (Fleetwood, 2011, p. 6). Illuminating
the ways that Black folk "grew," Jordan again creates an intervention into the
racial discourse which would distort or demonize Blackness. This Blackness
"fills in space between matter, between object and subject, between bodies,
between looking and being looked upon," it grows beyond obliteration to
survive (Fleetwood, 2011, p. 6). It is here we wish to begin, reflecting on how
Black pleasurable embodiments reorient in particular heteronormative, white
supremacist, and pathology-centered gazes. This is not to say that our work
exists solely as resistant to dominant gazes, but rather that as a cultural practice
and product, our performances of pleasure within *BoD* provide information
about how and what we come to know about the Black body, particularly a
Blackqueer body in and on its own terms.

Our enactments of pleasure in the performance also reveal a subversion – our pleasure is our survival. Survival, as Alexis Pauline Gumbs (2012) articulates, is "our living in the context of what we have overcome. Survival is life after disaster, life in honor of our ancestors, despite the genocidal forces worked against them specifically so we would not exist." Similarly, Lorde offers another vision of survival for the Black body. Speaking to women specifically, Lorde connects Black survival to the erotic, "as an assertion of the lifeforce of women; of that creative energy empowered, the knowledge and use of which we are now reclaiming in our language, our history, our dancing, our loving, our work, our lives" (Lorde, 1984, p. 55). Taken together, to grow is to survive and to survive is to cultivate the erotic within.

DEEP CREATION HAPPENS WITH/IN THE FEMININE: A LESSON

Here it is important to note that one of the lessons we learned from our performance was about the knowledge created from Black bodies when centered in pleasure. This knowledge was two-part for us, that to create knowledge about Blackness that might reorient pervasive misrepresentations of Blackness requires us to affirm the "yes within ourselves" (Lorde, 1984, p. 57), and by doing so, to say "'yes' to the 'female' within" (Spillers, 1987, p. 80). To affirm the yes within means to live in a way which connects us to the deepest parts of ourselves, our joys, our desires, and opens up bridges for others to share in that which brings us pleasure. This is no easy feat, as Lorde highlights, since,

> We have been raised to fear the *yes* within ourselves, our deepest cravings. But, once recognized, those which do not enhance our future lose their power and can be altered. The fear of our desires keeps them suspect and indiscriminately powerful, for to suppress any truth is to give it strength beyond endurance. The fear that we cannot grow beyond whatever distortions we may find within ourselves keeps us docile and loyal and obedient, externally defined, and leads us to accept many facets of our oppression as women. (Lorde, 1984, pp. 57–58)

In our performance of pleasure, our bodily enactment of our deepest joys and desires were used to create bridges between us and the audience, beginning with our internal directives. To say yes meant that I used my body to personally connect and disorient. My choice to make elongated eye contact with various women-presenting individuals while performing "Transcendental Sex," a poem written about the nerdy ways I flirt, "firmly rub Lucille, Harriet, Maya, Octavia, and Zora into my right palm," was a means of engaging the erotic. A sensual touch of this style is more properly considered an ancestral conjuring. As a queer individual, this flirtatious gesture is imagined, while writing it, to be exchanged with a woman but did not (necessarily) occlude others. Importantly, it symbolized a powerful connection mediated by a simple invitation, a handshake. Willing to risk the possibility of them presuming I am sexually summoning them (though I was inviting them to connect), this extended eye contact is to ensure they know I see them, that I recognize their power. And while the poem itself was about sex, it was *really* about how to create intimacy with someone spiritually. To say yes in this moment was to look deeply into and at women in that room to generate a deep connection, one that might also incite discomfort and even arousal.

To say yes also meant that I connected my body and desires with those in the room. For instance, when performing "American Dilemma," I allow the collage to be my shadow. Standing directly in front of the projected image of a young Black child, standing erect with one leg atop a mountain, their head dawning the American flag, draped in the curtains of the oval office during the Obama years, our Black bodies are transfixed. I, in the shadow of the image, the image in my own shadow as we both occupy the space of Alabama soil. My Black, queer body declaring love openly for Black boys/men, affirming our existence in my desire to "find the sweeeeeeetest chocolate boy/hold him close/and whisper sweet somethings in his ear/all night till morning," against the lone figure of a Black body looking out over the horizon, or perhaps turning their back and face away from "the promised land," away from the land which might maim them, which might thief away their life like it did Mike Brown. And yet here I stand, flat-footed, looking into the expanse of the audience, holding myself in place and wrapped in my own embrace to affirm the yes within myself that desires that I and other Blackqueer people live beyond annihilation. Off-setting narratives of the "absent Black father" or the emasculated male, Black men are found present and soft, maternal and paternal, loving and tender, because "tonight all the chocolate boys are hugging their chocolate babies a little closer/counting the blessings of breath/heart beats." Moving deeper into the audience, I close the scene with a loud whisper, a "yes within" imparted in this scene from a loved one to a child. The "revolt" that closes the scene is not only a recognition of my own deepest desires, to love Blackness beyond death, in survival, but to impart that love and desire to future generations in same-sex configurations and as a love that grounds all interactions. Moreover, this revolt is a birthright, to say yes to the "female within." This is to say,

the black American male embodies the *only* American community of males which has had the specific occasion to learn *who* the female is within itself, the infant child who bears the life against the could-be fateful gamble, against the odds of pulverization and murder, including her own. It is the heritage of the *mother* that the African-American male must regain as an aspect of his own personhood – the power of "yes" to the "female" within. (Spillers, 1987, p. 80)

Spillers (1987) and Lorde (1984) provide a means to consider how survival necessitates saying yes to ourselves and to the erotic forces, the feminine energy, deep connection, the female within who survives a multitude of erasures – erasure of self, patriarchal erasure, anti-Black erasure, capitalist erasure, heteronormative erasure, etc.

Through *Bodies on Display*, we cast our bodies up as living interventions into the field of vision that exists as a discourse, a set of actions, significations, and attachments which have material consequences for bodies racialized as Black. This is further explored in this chapter as we reflect upon temporal and context-specific articulations which were reflected back to us. In this process of casting, forecasting, and recasting our bodies for ourselves, the stage, and now the page (Spry, 2011), we are made to consider how,

Blackness does not only reside in the theatrical fantasy of the white imaginary that is then projected onto black bodies, nor is it always consciously acted out; rather, it is also the inexpressible yet undeniable racial experience of black people – the ways in which the "living of blackness" becomes a material way of knowing. (Johnson, 2003a, p. 8)

Within this performance and the offering of the pleasure section, Blackness, queerness, and pleasure were being remade. Diamond (1996) states, "'Re' acknowledges the preexisting discursive field, the repetition – and the desire to repeat…materializing something that exceeds our knowledge, that alters the shape of sites and imagines other as yet unsuspected modes of being" (pp. 1–2). Said in another way, the process and productive of Black pleasure forged new ways of seeing these concepts and locations, as well as their relationships anew.

REORIENTING THE GAZE: NOTES ON PLEASURE
AND BLENDED SCRIPTING

Broadly, the work of Hill L. Waters (HLW) involves gaze shifting and distortion. Comprising two Black, queer, cisgender-presenting individuals who practice fluid gender expressions, we foreground our work in assemblages of race, gender, and sexuality. Our decision to be a formalized collective, to be seen side-by-side and in relation, disrupts popular images, discourses, and configurations of race and sexuality collectivity as happening in homogenous gender formations. We recognized their monovisuality and sought to offer a different image. Describing the visual work of gender, performance theorist Elin Diamond (1996) states,

> It's not just that gender is culturally determined and historically contingent, but rather that "it" doesn't exist unless it's being done… Gender, then, is both a doing – a performance that puts conventional gender attributes into possibly disruptive play – and a thing done – a preexisting oppressive category. (pp. 4–5)

Thereby, HLW employs our individual bodies to do and disrupt gender, while simultaneously, our bodies together in sight of one another do this and other work. Specifically, it forces people to see queerness as a sexed and gendered endeavor, but not exclusively non-binary/gender neutral, male/masculine, female/feminine. Also, it requires that queerness be mitigated through bodies also Black or differentially hued. Applying this to *Bodies on Display*, our bodies stand in as object of the subjects of Blackness, queerness, Black pain, and in this particular chapter, Black pleasure. Concurrently, they function as objects objecting their abstraction, or what Tuck and Yang (2014) deem "performative examples of refusal" (p. 813).

In our collective practice, we also assume the labor of reorienting the gaze through what I have come to call Blended Scripting (Callier, 2013, 2016). Integral to our creation of performance text, Blended Scripting actualizes an alternative meaning-making practice (Hong & Ferguson, 2011) that places the researchers' narratives alongside those of other subjects, popular discourse surrounding the surveyed phenomena, and other relevant texts (e.g., visual display, media clips, music, fiction). The result is the creation of a complex, coherent, artistic representation of Black and queer youth lives and experiences. It is through this practice that we have come to learn ways to reaffirm the existence of Black, queer lives and desires. Further, the emancipatory space of performance embodied within the practice opens up possibilities to traverse the affective terrain associated with Black joy and trauma, while also providing a space to practice and imagine justice, intervening (if just for a moment) in the violence against our bodies.

Blended Scripting emerged from my research on youth of color experiences with violence and was sharpened through the collectivized practice of working with and for Black girls in SOLHOT. As a methodology, Blended Scripting engages in the purposeful juxtaposition of data (e.g., personal narrative, poetry, journal entries, personal communication) against other textual data sites (e.g., narratives, fiction, electronic/print media sources, music) in which performance, cultural memory, embodied knowledge, and personal narrative all come together to realize a text. This practice of moving research data into a dramatized form is in conversation with the following qualitative research methodologies: autoethnography (Alexander, 2011; Boylorn, 2013b; Brown, 2009, 2013; Chang, 2008; Durham, 2014; Holman Jones, Adams, & Ellis, 2013; McClaurin, 2001), performance methodology (Castagno, 2001; Denzin, 2003; Jones, 1997; Saldaña, 2011), Black performance (DeFrantz & Gonzalez, 2014), Black feminist performance (Anderson, 2008; Mahone, 1994; Shange, 1977), ethnodrama (Saldaña, 2005), and disruptive inquiry (Brown et al., 2014).

Informed by Black feminist theater practices, Shange's choreopoem (1977), Wreckless Theatrics as articulated by Brown (2013), and through SOLHOT and performance ethnography and autoethnography (Anderson, 2008; Jones, 1997), we utilize Blended Scripting as a means to break and remake form. We break forms which might disappear the nuanced, complex lives of Black people in order to remake forms which reappear the Black body, Black joy, genius, and freedom (Brown, personal communication, 2016). Where traditional archives fail, Blended Scripting has proven useful in valuing the lives and stories of Black, queer people. It has shown up as love, an antidote to death, a means to create value, and a way to hold the lives of Black, queer people as intrinsically valuable.

This is illustrated within the excerpt from *BoD*, "Pleasure," and specifically through the piece entitled, "Touch Me Here/Good Lovin." After Miguel soulfully sings, "I need some real good lovin', 'cause I'm troubled by the things that I see," we begin the scene with the words uttered by Hill and an overlapped response from Waters:

HILL:	WATERS:
when looking at myself after a shower reading sonia, lucille, audre, zora watching her long to be touched nipple biting first time, all of them	touch me here and here leave your mark right here

The juxtaposition and interplay of the music, words, and bodies on stage create a moment in which the Black, queer body in joy and ecstasy is centered. As a creative practice, Blended Scripting traverses the affective terrains of Black, queer joy and trauma, and invites audiences alongside the performers to consider love and lovin – the act of making love – as central to the care of and for Black people, a queer act and a necessity as we hold the weight of being "troubled by the things that I see." The care for and of echoes love as a verb. As feminist scholar bell hooks states, "When we understand love as the will to nurture our own and another's spiritual growth, it becomes clear that we cannot claim to love if we are hurtful and abusive" (hooks, 2000, p. 6).

CONCLUSION

To love Blackness, Black people, and the Black body asks us to be troubled by the things that we see, a la Miguel, to refrain from harm and abuse, and to actively seek out paths to nurture one another (Johnson, Jackson, Stovall, & Baszile, 2017). Moving beyond the body as a site of harm, embodied performances of Blackness allow entryways to note and redress harm in complicated ways. Tactically, performance is an intimate space to speak Blackness into its own existence, a space to imagine and practice freedom, a space for unbridled Black pleasures. Moreover, performance offers a way for bodily knowledge to be placed front-and-center and for the knowledge created between the performers and audience to be made available to both. In the case of pleasure and Blackqueer bodies, *BoD* demands that audiences wrestle with their pleasures, longings, and what parts Blackness and queerness does or does not play in them. Within our larger collective practice as artist-scholars, we turn to performance as a way to conjure new, different worlds through visual renderings that center Blackness as expansive and inclusive.

Further, pleasure created by and through Black bodies is deeply tied to sovereignty and education. Yet, their relationship is not easily parsed out or intelligible. This is because, as Dillard (2016) provides for us, sovereignty is about self-definition, in which schools and educative sites set up the possibilities for embracing and declaring our sense of self. Moreover, it is about Black people decidedly insisting that we matter, that our education matters, and that our education must be about more than conventional measures of academic achievement. Instead, that our education must include and exceed self-concept to living out our full humanity. To do so embraces the possibility of education as sovereignty in which Black people "live and love by thinking and being beyond the definitions given to us and about us" (Dillard, 2016, p. 212). Within an educational context that often does more harm than good to Black communities and children, sovereignty is risky business and can be aided if educators in schools and our society in general would only ask, "Who and what do you see when you see Black people?" and "How do Black lives matter to our work – and how would Black people see that they matter in our work?" (Dillard, 2016, p. 212).

This is the labor-embodied performances of pleasure taken up within *Bodies on Display*. Invited into this space of nurture, the performers provide a window of seeing lovin in action. The photos selected demonstrate this intention, our eyes peering back to you. See us as we also see ourselves. Notice how the images allow us to watch you as you watch us. *BoD* is an invitation to see Blackness and pleasure on their own terms, in complex, queer fullness. A capitalist ideal of voyeuristic consumptive pornography is both unwarranted and futile.

HILL: I feel the most free where…

i see beautiful Blackness staring back at me…

REFLECTION QUESTIONS & INTERACTIVE EXERCISE

General Questions

- While reading this chapter, what meaning did you make between the words on the page and the photographs?
- How did our actual bodies correspond with your construction of our Black queerness?

For Educators

- How do you look for signs of Blackness and queerness in your educational space? What are the signs and symbols you deem representative of Blackness, queerness, and Blackqueerness?
- In what ways do their importance show up in your pedagogy, content, etc.?

Shifting the Gaze

Directions: Choose one photograph from Chapter 2 as your focus. Once you have decided which picture to use, examine the image for two minutes and quickly choose words and brief phrases to describe it. Be sure to focus your undivided attention on the person in the picture. Then, choose one corner of the picture to direct your gaze. Stay in that corner for some time (one minute or so) and slowly begin to scale out, making your visibility of the picture widen. Once you get to the face of a person, stop and write what you noticed. If you choose a picture with multiple faces, you can choose to engage how you make sense of one face based on its relation to the other or simply choose one face to give your focused attention. Specifically, focus on which part of the face you noticed first. Now, begin at the bottom of the page and slowly make your way up the page until you get to someone's eyes. Once there, stop scanning and look in their eyes for 30 seconds or so. Write down how this felt. Upon completion of engaging these different perspectives, reflect upon the process using the following questions: What did you notice? Which angle of looking created the most discomfort, and why? How important was the space surrounding the face and body of person? What did this activity teach you about gaze?

ACKNOWLEDGEMENT

All photographs within this chapter, except for the collage, "The American Dilemma," were used with permission from the photographer Jonathan Norris. Special thanks to him for beautifully capturing us in motion and on the fly.

NOTES

[1] How to read this performance: Cast of characters include Hill and Waters, who are the artists and creators of the live art installation. Other characters include EzB and P. Parker, who serve as docents – educational guides – leading the audience through the museum. The distinguishing factors between the docents, the artists, and live art were subtle, with the docents wearing suit jackets, utilizing notecards, and announcing their position within the museum when delivering lines. Your reading will intentionally be stretched as you are challenged to take in and make sense of our words from the performance, the images from the performance, and the performativity of each on the page. The overall impact may feel disorienting, but it is intended to reorient how you see and read Black bodies, how you hold the weight of imagery and the simultaneity of voice and sound together. Here, we are asking you to reconsider our vocabulary and the way we make sense of the world through our visual and culturally embedded reading practices.

[2] Docents serve as guides throughout the performance. Similar to museum guides, our docents provide important information and knowledge to the audience as they travel through the live museum. They inform the audience of the artist name, title and medium of the art work, as well as other relevant educational information. The docent's speaking text has been indented when it is specifically about the piece the audience is about to view.

[3] Informed by Shange (1977), each piece rendered and their whole together manifests a choreopoem. The music anchoring each piece is left intentionally as a part of the script for audiences who might read this text to gain an understanding of the texture of each piece.

[4] Articulated by Ruth Nicole Brown (2013), visionary of SOLHOT, "to homegirl [and homeboy] is to commit to a very sincere practice of remembering Black girlhood as a way to honor oneself and to practice the selflessness necessary to honor someone else, remembered whole" (p. 47). To assume the position of homegirl/boy is to accept responsibility for creating space for being and breathing on our own terms and to recognize when others as we ourselves need resuscitation.

[5] The image and poem highlighted in this chapter are known together within the performance as the "American Dilemma." The image itself is a collage created by Callier (2015), which is projected as a slideshow during this scene in the performance.

3. LOOKING AGAIN

Collective Visions, Collective Sight/Seeing

Is that how we look to you
a partial nothing clearly real?
(Jordan, 1969, p. 4)

I dreamed about a space where Black girls would not be an afterthought. Would not exist in comparison. Would not be watched for the purpose of punishment or voyeurism. I thought about a space where we as Black girls would be engaged, not bored. Surely, I felt, in this space we would not have to carry the weight of the world in or with us. I did not want us to assemble to become empowered, or to become anything really. I wanted a space for Black girls to be together and have fun. If such a space could exist and Black girlhood could be deployed as an organizing construct, I realized that it would be political and revolutionary. (Brown, 2013, p. 39)

In my mind, I screamed, "save yourself first!" When you address your own issues without trying to save others from theirs, then and only then will you be able to help others. […] In SOLHOT, we recognize that it is imperative that we all actively engage in self-reflection for the sake of black girlhood celebration and personal well-being. (Garner, 2011)

"Check-In" is a tone-setter, a temperature check, to see what is pressing on each of our hearts and minds, and to clue each other in on what has happened that day and/or since we last saw each other. Sometimes our check-ins are short. For instance, "Check-In, I'm here, Check-Out." Sometimes, they are longer rants, revealing our humanity back to ourselves, righting some wrong that happened earlier in our day, or spilling the latest tea about what's happening in our lives. For instance,

Check-In: It's Dom here, y'all. It's been a minute since I've checked in with y'all formally, but I do so in my head and heart often. Come to think about it, I been checking in since 2008, but back then, I wasn't fully present to this exercise, this ritual that sets the tone for everyone coming together to make SOLHOT that day. Back then, I was too busy trying to keep it all together to even hint at the possibility of being

© KONINKLIJKE BRILL NV, LEIDEN, 2019 | DOI:10.1163/9789004392243_004

exactly what I was: a mess. But as my great-granny BJ would say, there is always tomorrow and tomorrow is today for me. Right now, I am floating; I'm taking more seriously my everyday joy and less seriously the consequences of not taking yourself too seriously. I am steeped in love and give it everywhere I go. I'm also open to physical intimacy. This is really new, especially since my beautiful romantic partnership transitioned into a beautiful transcending best friendship. I say I'm floating because I am taking time to know me more deeply, appreciate all around me, clarify things I desire, and decide if the desire is strong enough to pursue. Real talk, at this moment, I'm most deeply committed to my freedom journey and professionally producing the work that matters to me and that ultimately lands me in a spot unthinkable because it was made with me – present and future me – in mind. Here's to being more than okay with who I am and where I am today. Check-In, Check-Out.

Check-In: Heyyyy y'all, it's me Durell, AKA Cake Baker, AKA Song of Solomon, S.O.S – the names you gave me in our community together. Friends bring friends to SOLHOT and this is our story. Cha Cha and Candy, in true SOLHOT fashion you invited me in to work with and for Black girls, Black people, us, and I've been hangin ever since that first rehearsal for "The Rhythm, The Rhyme, and The Reason"[1] back in summer 2008. Something new and different happens in our deciding to come together, in choosing each other over and over again at the edge of our battles;[2] we become each other's keepers, chosen family, witnesses, a collective. Whatever the words, we hold on to each other and not the idea of what our coming together could mean.[3] For that I am grateful, and in the words of Klevah, "never let me go."[4] Check-Out!

In essence, this activity utilizes Black girl vernacular to touch base about what is sustaining us, challenging us, weighing on us, ailing us, and healing us. Created by SOLHOT homegirl, Sheri, "The process of Check-In resembles free styling in a cipher: narratives are built off of other narratives; there is a call-and-response type of structure to it" (Garner, 2012, p. 231). Extending its original intention, we use "Check-In" here as a means of publicly naming who we be and how we have taken up and expanded the work of SOLHOT. To be Black, queer, and (eternal) students of SOLHOT is to constantly check-in with ourselves and each other about our ongoing practices of love, Black feminism, and how we work with youth broadly and Black girls specifically.

Extending the work of and our work in SOLHOT that challenge tropes and conventional gazes afforded to Black girls, this chapter elucidates how organizing within and around an organic intergenerational Black feminist approach shifts how Black girls are seen, and uncovers the personal work necessary to work with youth in affirming and ethical ways. Beginning with Brown and the work of SOLHOT, to reorient our relationship to Black girls involves marking Black girlhood as celebration, which Brown (2009) insists, "requires that I never define what Black girlhood means or what successful celebration looks like – by myself. The significance of Black girlhood celebration is building on what we have learned as Black girls and women and then liberating ourselves from it" (Brown, 2009, p. 22). Rather than steeping these subjects in cemented locations and the language of research and external gazing, she shifts the orientation of studies, Black Girlhood Studies (BGS) to be exact, to be rooted in celebration. In doing so, Brown recognizes and subverts the confinement of Black girls and Black girlhood as subjects to be objectified as an area of study for others to gaze upon and write *about.* In declaring it celebration, Brown sets the tone for those seeking to engage BGS – a celebration must be found in the work.

Revamping the terms that guide scholarship and research in the name of seeing the subject as subject and the subject as valuable in and of itself is a similar approach taken by Critical Youth Studies scholars. Critical Youth Studies emerges as a novel area committed generally to innovative and less hierarchical ways of studying the lived experience of youth (Ibrahim & Steinberg, 2014). Respective of their differing genealogies, Black Girlhood Studies and Critical Youth Studies emerge as intentional interventions into popular discourse on who youth are and their situatedness as consumers of knowledge and culture, and expands the ideas of which youth are worth studying (Talbert, 2014). In addition, they transgress traditionally bounded categories (i.e., girl, youth) to blur the lines between youth, child, and adult, as well as girl and woman. With interdisciplinary foundations and commitments, the labor of Black Girlhood Studies and Critical Youth Studies involves rightfully naming youth, with a focus on Black girls in the former field, as best suited to speak to, problem solve, and imagine their lived experiences. Here, we name and briefly outline their relationship as a means of drawing connections between Youth Studies, a field largely responsible for youth development and which has connections to programming models for youth, and Black Girlhood Studies, a field that subverts, denies, and critiques Youth Studies, as well as the theoretical and methodological discussions thereafter on youth spaces, agency, and empowerment.

Just because I'm Black doesn't mean i'm dumb

Just because I look mean doesn't mean i'm mean

Just because I don't smile doesn't mean...

Just because I'm quiet doesn't mean...

Just because I...

During this communal process, we laugh, flex,[5] listen, nod heads in agreement, read "Just Because" statements for those unwilling and/or too shy to vocally participate, and encourage those insistent that "I don't know what to say" to simply offer up something. In this collective experience, homegirls/boys and li'l homies set the record straight. In SOLHOT, we get to, like Sammus,[6] participate in "mighty morphing" and defy the narrow perceptions imposed upon us.

As an extension of our work in SOLHOT, this chapter elucidates what organizing within and around an organic intergenerational Black feminist approach can shift in how to work *with* youth, and what is differently possible in doing so. In this chapter, we argue that working with youth, and in particular Black girls, requires epistemic and methodological reorientations that situate the body, and thus the cultures inhabited by these bodies, as an integral site of learning and the space from which our political actions with youth springs forth. Through narrative and critical reflection, this chapter invites read(er)s into a reorienting process of working in true collaboration *with* youth, in particular Black girls. Specifically, this chapter moves through two cases, or what we call "lessons." These lessons illustrate how the collective organizing strategies of SOLHOT center Black girls' ways of knowing, expand our views of them, create Black girl spaces of celebration, and foster new ways of working *with* and *for* youth. Lastly, we close with final thoughts on how we can create more life-affirming practices for Black youth, and demonstrate how SOLHOT contributes to both theoretical and methodological discussions on youth organizing, agency, empowerment, resistance, and space.

SOLHOT LESSON I: "JUST BECAUSE...DON'T MEAN..."

Just because I _____

doesn't mean I _____

My name is _____

And I am _____

(Brown, 2009, p. 58)

In SOLHOT, "Just Because" is an exercise enacted at the start of a session. Introduced by SOLHOT homegirl Joelle, it "intentionally provide[s] a complex self-definition of who we are in spite of people's first impression," stereotypes, and perceptions (Brown, 2009, p. 58). Further, it provides a snapshot of the ways Black girls and others present, refute, respond to, and internalize external valuations. Each person in attendance completes the statement by filling in the blanks, and then everyone shares with the collective. Laughter, silence, smiles, and stories are often engendered from these statements. As pedagogy, "Just Because" invites us all to simultaneously be teacher and student. It demands that we practice Black feminism and enact principles of Black girlhood celebration by embracing paradox, holding competing narratives in tandem, and centering Black girl truths (Brown, 2009). "Just Because" functions as a unit of organization and analysis. By sharing our own critical memories of it, we offer here insights into how it demonstrates and questions assumptions about youth organizing, subjectivity, agency, and resistance.

If taken at face value without deeper prodding, "Just Because" can seem like a great icebreaker. This is part of what the opening ritual does: reacquaints us with one another and catches us up on each other's daily lives. But this SOLHOT ritual is much more than that. As witnesses and participants, we note how it functions as a way for the girls and those assembled to (i) affirm themselves and their identities, (ii) create a space of autonomy, and (iii) offer up counternarratives to the scripts often placed on and against their Black girl bodies. Or, as Brown (2009) states, "This activity has allowed us to name ourselves as individuals, to reveal personal contradictions, to share deep secrets, to validate those identities that are meaningful, and to create a group identity that recognizes and celebrates our diversity" (p. 58).

It is striking how "Just Because" asks educational researchers, teachers, and witnesses to Black brilliance and Black girl genius to examine what Black girls are trying to tell us. Their frequent refusal to be seen as mean, or dumb, or shy, or loud are responses to the ways Black girls experience school and life. According to a 2015 African-American Policy Forum report, the first to highlight Black girls' experiences in educational spaces, Black girls are suspended and expelled at disproportionate rates. Moreover, they endure over-policing of their bodies and behavior. This report illustrates the lack of support and protection generally provided to Black girls in formal educational settings. However, what we know through "Just Because," because a Black girl told us so and we believed her, is *how* their bodies are regulated (Brown, 2009, 2013). Regulated, to be seen as incapable of producing knowledge.

Through the practice of "Just Because," we have learned that we must create space for Black girls, listen to the stories they tell us, and then act/react accordingly. For instance, when a Black girl reveals to us and confirms (as we know) that "they are not dumb," we believe them. In SOLHOT, not only do we believe them, but we continue to be moved by this knowingness to reflect the girls' genius back to them. How we affirm that the Black girl, who has trouble with writing or reading and who wants us to know that she is not dumb because people mistake her Black girlness as such, has genius and value takes on a variety of modes. Sometimes, it's through our creation of arts-based, embodied pedagogy that might allow for this same girl to lead an activity that day. Sometimes, it's the immediate response of a homegirl/boy, "Nah you ain't." Sometimes, it's from the girls who ask that same girl, who they know is a skilled dancer, singer, poet, lyricist, or rapper, to sing, dance, or rap for us. In SOLHOT, our pre-planned curriculum is always a guide and therefore is easily adjusted for these (unexpected) moments. The girls' wants or needs are not an interruption or disruption to our learning together; it is in fact the education we are seeking to create. Through our practice of "Just Because," we have found a way to center Black girls and their stories, a way in which they create their own narratives about themselves and their lives, a way for us to affirm each other, to resist the things that are untrue about us, to accept the inconvenient truths about ourselves, and to begin to shift power dynamics created by institutions that do not have our well-being in mind.

"Just Because" is exercise, pedagogy, and lesson. As a lesson, it teaches that just because homegirls/boys devised the curriculum for a given day doesn't mean it will be carried out that day or at all. Just because homegirls/boys are older doesn't mean we aren't working through similar issues as the girls. Just because our intentions are good doesn't mean it always shows up in our work. In our work and through continued engagement with "Just Because," we learn that doing work that intends to routinely and consistently meet the needs of all is difficult, if not impossible. And yet, just because such intentions are lofty and seemingly unrealistic doesn't mean we don't consistently aspire to defy this impossibility with creative potential (Brown, 2013; University of Illinois Press, 2013).

Lastly, through "Just Because," we know that making space for Black girls to *be* also requires enigmatic pedagogy where the coming together and the chorale of Black girlhoods and Black girl realities create the narrative. It is important then, that researchers, educators, and those invested in working with youth mind the very ways in which we co-organize youth spaces, create space for their autonomous action, listen to them, and respond in kind. It is in this vein that what has come to be affectionately described as "dirty work" is outlined and in relationship to its complex kin, Wreckless Theatrics. As signifiers of the labor that advocates, organizers, and other older and possibly elder individuals working with Black girls must do to show up and be fully present, "dirty work" and "Wreckless Theatrics" adjust the lens for it to shine not on the girls but on those who say they are here for the girls.

SOLHOT LESSON II: SAVE YOURSELF FIRST: RECOLLECTING *DIRTY WORK* AND WRECKLESS THEATRICS

V1: This work is dirty work

Because you make it be…

If only you reverenced me…

Gesture appropriate pronoun

V2: If only you reverenced her

V3: If only you reverenced us

V1: Listened to me…

V2: Listened to her

V1: Held me when I cried…

V3: Held her when she cried

V1: Loved me as I needed…

V2: Loved us as we needed

V3: Loved her as she needed

V1: Heard me…

V3: Heard her

All: Saw

V1: me

V2: her

V3: us

All: whole, talented, beautiful, and a divine gift…

V1: And so *we*

V3: And so *we*

V2: And so *we*

V1: do this cleansing work, this exorcism of demons which rack our bodies, hold captive our minds, silence our tongues, and allow you to see us as deaf, dumb, and blind…

The above excerpt comes from a performance created in conversation with Black girls and those who love them. Originally a poem, "Dirty Work" signified my "ethnographic notes," where I first began making sense of the reorientation that Black girls and Black girlhood demands regarding how to do youth organizing work, particularly as it relates to working *with* youth in educational spaces (Callier 2008). Note that both the poem and performance are interchangeably referred to as "Dirty Work," though our analysis is primarily focused on the performance of the poem and the preceding excerpt. To further examine how the performance engages with methodologies that offer windows into youth culture, it is important to begin with a primary epistemological lens that drives and derives from our work with Black girls.

In SOLHOT, we are guided by the understanding that Black girls are knowledge creators. "Dirty Work" echoes one of the core tenets of SOLHOT: to save yourself first. As SOLHOT homegirl, Garner (2011), states,

> […] how SOLHOT differs from most girl groups, we are not in the practice of girl saving. In the vein of "saving yourself first," volunteers in SOLHOT do not come into the space with the misconceived notion that the issues we face are more important than those the girls face. Nor do we enter the space trying to hide our concerns. If we do enter the space believing that our issues are more important, that we have all the answers or trying to hide our own struggles, SOLHOT will become unproductive and stagnant. SOLHOT cannot and will not function fully unless our truths are revealed, acknowledged and respected.

When we enter SOLHOT, we bring with us our baggage, our being, and the reasons we need saving. In SOLHOT, as expressed by homegirl Porshe, we are in the practice of being together, problem solving together, and speaking our multiple, contradictory, and at times conflicting truths (Garner, 2011). This is the labor of Black girlhood celebration (Brown, 2009) and the work of articulating Black girlhood in public, academic, and other spaces outside of our sacred meeting grounds. More than just a way to organize, to enter work with Black girls, deem it celebration, and posit unlearning and self-saving as core is to epistemologically ground working *with* Black girls in paradox. In this way, we enter relationships of knowledge creation that require us to be in relationship with one another. Moreover, we are guided not by hierarchical systems of knowledge production, but come to the space seeing the girls and ourselves as co-generators of knowledge. In our coming together, we know what can change our world. To do so also means that we are not saviors or mentors of any sort, but rather that we are coproducing knowledge, co-teachers and witnesses to each other's genius (Brown, 2013). This is fundamental to SOLHOT's practice, given the fact that Black girls are rarely assumed to be knowledge producers or even experts of their own lives (Brown, 2014).

As the poem illustrates, one of the ways we coproduce knowledge and bear witness to the girls' genius is through performance. Here, we wish to share methodology that comes out of SOLHOT. As a means of illuminating and embracing wrecklessness as a creative and productive space in the lives of Black girls and women, Brown (2014) offers "Wreckless Theatrics." Brown (2009) asserts, "SOLHOT is all about the messy in-between – yes you can, no you don't have to, and please think about doing it again – that we have ciphered off into different projects with specific aims" (p. 131). Wreckless Theatrics, then, is an artistic paradigm that functions as a communally based arbiter, one which holds in tandem various and rubbing voices and experiences of Black girlhood that demand a new way of seeing Black girls and Black girlhood, that commands those invested in social justice to think more complexly about the journey and practice of freedom (Brown, 2014).

Wreckless Theatrics is a research methodology in conversation with performance methodology, auto/ethnography, hip-hop theater aesthetics, hip-hop feminist art and pedagogy, and Black feminist performance, and asserts that research should be a collaborative and collective knowledge-production process. Tenets of the practice include embracing the dramatic structuring of everyday life, highlighting the motions and emotions of Black girls in living their lives, sharing the stories of Black girlhood as told by

Black girls and those who love them, creating, representing, and presenting culturally embodied knowledge, particularly of Black girls, and valuing the cultural resources and performances of Black girlhood. It is rooted in collective action and is dedicated to the survival of Black girls everywhere.

Like many of the things created in SOLHOT, individually at first but made of collective use and in relationship to a collective, "Dirty Work" is no different. It has become a staple over the years, one of our manifestos for working with Black girls, for working with and for each other as a collective. In the doing, reciting, and performing of "Dirty Work," it has become our dare to each other and our reminder of what working *with* Black girls in affirming ways requires. Simultaneously, it serves as a warning to others who think they are working for Black girls' liberation, freedom, and Black girlhood celebration, but who are really stuck on mentoring, policing, and refining Black girls into respectable ladies. As the poem suggests, our work is one in which "many are called but few are chosen." The poem and performance have continued to teach us that the grime of this labor is often brought in by us, those adults well-intentioned and trained in the politics of standards, respectability, and self-policing. Black girls continue to educate those of us willing to save ourselves on how to practice freedom. In turn, we generate new perspectives and make space for new ways of working alongside Black girls and youth.

Warm cheeks, deer-in-headlights stare, perspiring hands, and momentary paralysis – this was my physiological response during a homegirl session dedicated to addressing their curiosities about sex, and specifically orgasms. In the moment I wondered: In a middle school? How we gonna talk about sex in a middle school? How did the girls catch wind of the word orgasm? Were we going to use the word orgasm in our lesson? The session was amazing and turned into a series of sessions connected to sexuality, including one on naming your vagina. Afterwards, I recounted my trepidation, what I expressed in the session (very little), and what that said about my own sexuality or not. In this time of reflection, I (re)membered I had attended an all-girls, abstinence-only, Catholic high school, grew up being told to keep my pocketbook clean, and that I had developed curiosity about pleasure and its relationship to my "private parts" around age seven (apparently too young because I started to be called fas' for the questions I asked). Further, I had to remind myself that I had given my vagina a name in my early 20s to reclaim it, to forgive myself for the things uncontrollable that happened to it and other things that happened because I didn't feel it belonged to me.

Unknowingly, that homegirl planning session engendered an excavation. It started to exhume my body's sex narrative and pushed me to ask why sex was a topic I spoke little about publicly and an act for which I was only recently claiming autonomous authority. (Re)membering was painful, sobering, dirty work. Between this initial session and the next where we drew pictures of our vagina as we imagined them (sunshine, abstract image with lots of colors, rainfall, smiley face), this work began. It continues still. This is but one example of the importance of saving ourselves and doing so as homegirls/boys. In planning to bring a lesson the girls asked for, I was confronted with baggage initially misrecognized as concern about the so-called appropriateness of sex conversations in school. Today, this concern is laughable and points to the ways that who we are, what we learned, and how we learned come out in the wash when working with youth. If we fail to save ourselves in the process of working with youth and Black girls, we risk denying them of what they asked for, that which they know they need.

One of the core tenets of Wreckless Theatrics is that "it allows for the creation, presentation, and representations of culturally embodied knowledge of import to particular communities of practice" (Brown, 2014, p. 37). To create anything of use to someone else, it first has to be of use to ourselves. That is a hallmark of good poetry: it cannot tell lies, as June Jordan tells us (Muller and The Poetry for the People Blueprint Collective, 1995). Wreckless Theatrics builds on this history of poem/poet turned prophet/performer/ priestess as the frame of the choreopoems (Shange, 1977) demands that we might 'fess up to that which is killing us (Bambara, 1980).

In SOLHOT, grounded by Wreckless Theatrics, our performances of sex, sexuality, pleasure, and our deepest joys – the erotic, as Lorde (1984) calls it – are recurring themes we visit, revisit, and perform publicly. Often these public performances began as self-revelations, private promises to and for ourselves and in community with those who love us back. As the reflection above denotes, we move from the personal as political. How do we remain present and talk about sticky subjects? How do we work through our own stuff? How can we examine our own lives? How do we save ourselves first? These organizing dilemmas become the fertile ground through which Wreckless Theatrics allow us the ability to display our truths, our politics, and particularly the politics of the erotic in an aesthetic form. At its core, the only way we can bring the wreck is when and if we are deeply in relationship with ourselves, saving our own lives. Saving ourselves first means we need to ask ourselves hard questions.

Although there were years between the exercise of naming our vaginas and when we first performed revelations of that SOLHOT session and other ones that shed light on centering our own healing, the questions, the necessity of saving ourselves first in order to enact the embodied pedagogy

67

and knowledge of Wreckless Theatrics is ever present. How else can you perform the erotic on stage, how else could we ask the girls to name their vaginas if we couldn't locate our own deepest joys and longings, name our own vaginas, reclaim our own pleasures? During a class in which we were working on a script about our work in SOLHOT, Dr. B asked, "Do you know how to make love to yourself?" This was not in the pedestrian understanding of the pornographic, but a real question asking just how deep our love goes. By demanding that the representation and embodied knowledge created be of use to communities of practice, Wreckless Theatrics also reiterated that need for us to save ourselves first. This necessitated another tenet of the practice, another means of saving ourselves first: to "share stories of Black girlhood as told by Black girls and those who love them as a means of collective actions dedicated to the survival of Black girls everywhere." The dirty work of our truths, "revealed, acknowledged and respected" (Garner, 2011), moved through a performance method and aesthetic that demands the same qualities opens pathways for our collective survival generally, and more specifically for Black girls.

CONCLUSION

In working with Black girls, a group often marginalized and excluded from educational policymaking, spaces constructed with them at the fore must feel and call upon different aesthetic conditions. Who *looks* at Black girls, and when they do, what do they see? A problem to be fixed (Carroll, 1997; Lei, 2003; Morris, 2007), too much sass (Fordham, 1993; Jones, 2010; Lei, 2003; Winn, 2011), prime targets for street harassment (Callier, 2016; Fogg-Davis, 2006; Jones, 2010), second-class citizens (Cox, 2015; Morris, 2016; Winn, 2011), hypersexual (Sears, 2010), absences (Crenshaw, Ocen, & Nanda, 2015; Hill, 2014a; Lightfoot, 1976; Morris, 2016), the divine architects of contemporary popular culture (Durham, 2014; Gaunt, 2006; LaBennett, 2011), genius (Brown, 2013), resilience (Evans-Winters, 2005; Ladner, 1971; Stevens, 2002), the future (Jarmon, 2013)? What do you see? Saving Our Lives Hear Our Truths (SOLHOT) homegirl Asha French, like many of the other co-organizers of SOLHOT, knows and sees that "Black girls are free and Black girlhood is freedom" (French, 2012). Such sight/seeing requires a reorganizing of the scripts often used to see, know, and understand Black girls. This, as Black feminist forebearers have testified, is nothing short of political liberation. It asks of us as researchers, educators, and those invested in dismantling structures of domination in all their forms to activate ontological, epistemological, methodological, and political rigor, innovation, and commitment, which would center Blackness and Black girls in particular (Brown, 2009, 2013; Combahee River Collective, 1995; Dillard, 2012; Durham, 2014; Spillers, 1987; Walker, 1983; Wynter & McKittrick, 2015). In the more than ten years of its practice, SOLHOT has offered these tools, centering Black girl ways of knowing, their desires, needs, and freedom.

Through our continued practice of SOLHOT, we also learned a few ways to shift epistemological grounds that would situate Black girls and youth as knowledge producers and therefore experts on how to bring about the change they deem necessary in their own lives. We elucidated two practices that offer new methodological ways of working *with* and *for* youth. Wreckless Theatrics is one of the ways to begin to do this work. We hold fast to the idea that when Black girls are listened to, believed, and trusted, and when we decidedly work *with* them in a collective toward collaboration, power not only shifts, but the world itself is made anew, envisioned through the eyes of Black girls. As we began this chapter with the insight of June Jordan, on thinking about how we see Black youth, we close here again, asking us all to re-envision our sight. We must insist that we see Black youth and Black girls as "whole, talented, beautiful, and a divine gift" (Callier, 2008). By working alongside Black girls through the praxis of SOLHOT, we learn that in celebrating Black girls and Black girlhood, we have the potential to incite "cleansing work," labor that will change those learning to celebrate and reverberate across space and time.

REFLECTION QUESTIONS

General Questions

- In your life and work, what does "dirty work" look like?
- What is one piece of advice you are taking away from the chapter about working with Black girls and/or collective work?

For Educators

- In your teaching practice, how do you center the innate knowledge that Black girls and youth of color bring into your classrooms?
- In your teaching practice, how do you see Black girls?
- How do your teaching practices value the lives, experiences, and knowledge of youth of color broadly, and Black girls specifically?

NOTES

[1] The Rhythm, The Rhyme, and the Reason (RRR) was a performance text which debuted at the University of Illinois in Fall 2008. Based on ethnographic field notes and co-authored by SOLHOT homegirls Chamara Jewel Kwakye, Claudine Candy Taaffe, and Ruth Nicole Brown, RRR explores the complexities of Black girlhood and what it means to work with and for Black girls beyond the "girl saving" mentorships, initiatives, and programs. See Forrest (2009).

[2] In her poem, "Outlines," Lorde (1997a) states, "We have chosen each other/and the edge of each other's battles/the war is the same/if we lose/someday women's blood will congeal/upon a dead planet/if we win/there is no telling" (pp. 365–366). Choosing each other and the edge of each other's battles is our praxis of solidarity within SOLHOT, and represents a part of the ethos of being with and for Black girls.

[3] See We Levitate (2016), from their EP, *How I Feel*, "Take Care" (https://welevitate.bandcamp.com/album/how-i-feel-ep).

[4] See Klevah (2015) from her EP, *Golden*, "Good Lover" (https://soundcloud.com/klevah/klevah-golden-18-good-lover).

[5] According to the Urban Dictionary, to flex means to show off, gloat, boast, and/or to put up a front or facade. During "Just Because," flexin' can and does take on both of these properties and sometimes a combination of the two.

[6] In 2016, Sammus released her second single, "Mighty Morphing," and at SOLHOT's Black Girl Genius Week February that same year, it became the weekend's anthem. As a feminist and hip-hop head, Sammus crossed paths with members of SOLHOT years before she was invited to headline the hip-hop concert for the week. Paralleling SOLHOT's embrace of paradox, variety, and infinite as it pertains to what constitutes being a Black girl, "Mighty Morphing" claims heterogeneity, ever-evolving Black girl and woman ways of being, and the importance and quotidian genius of switching it up as Black girls and women. Declaring "I am more things than I'm reporting" is to also denounce the need to explain all parts of who she/we be to others while also reminding us that we are too much (and that is more than okay) to be reduced to thing or another. See video at https://binged.it/2Ix4Z6Q

4. ANSWERING THE CALL

Centering Spirit in Auto/Ethnography

With Freddie Gray heavy on our hearts and Sandra Bland dancing in our tears, we wrote what would become our second performance, *Bodies on Display: An Exploration of Love, Intimacy, Violence, and the Black, Queer Body* (Waters, 2015). We were moved deeply by the deaths of Black folk at the hands of police. We pondered when and where Black people could find time for pleasure in moments saturated in loss. Our foremothers knew and have provided some advice about how our scholarship could serve as knowing and remembering (Brown, 2009). To know and remember is a refrain and a ritual of SOLHOT Black girlhood worldmaking. In an incense circle, for example, SOLHOT presenters would stand around a candle and recall the name of person(s) to know and remember. As auto/ethnographers committed to this ritual as part of our individual scholarship and collective practice, we offered *Bodies on Display* as enactment and a call to attend to the high stakes of Black bodies performing collaborative qualitative research.

Since the deaths of Freddie and Sandra, we continue to grapple with sociocultural displays of the Black body and how autoethnography might respond to these displays. We ask: Where are Black youth in auto/ethnography? What is education (K-12) missing when not taking a vested interest in auto/ethnography? What would a conversation between the field of education, an auto/ethnographic-informed performance, and a Black feminist ethos look like? In this chapter, we argue for centering Black girl worldmaking and Black women's sensibilities as they refashion the "I" in autoethnography. Moreover, we note how this shift illuminates the potentiality of bridges between autoethnography and education, especially as it pertains to divestment in Blackness as spectacle only. Specifically, we illustrate this by demonstrating how autoethnography is shifted through Black girl worldmaking and Black women's sensibilities, which redefine the "I" in autoethnography while integrating and centering spiritual ways of knowing within an otherwise "heady" form of inquiry and methodological approach.

© KONINKLIJKE BRILL NV, LEIDEN, 2019 | DOI:10.1163/9789004392243_005

THE CONTRIBUTION OF AUTO/ETHNOGRAPHY
TO QUALITATIVE RESEARCH

Autoethnography as a methodology has given a great deal to the field of qualitative research. It troubles the waters between participating and observing (Behar, 1996; Boylorn, 2013a; Brown, 2009; Spry, 2016), writing about research and writing about the self (McClaurin, 2012), naming yourself and naming others within the narrative or performance (Anderson, 2006; Bochner & Ellis, 2016; Callier, Hill, & Waters, 2017a; Jones, Adams, & Ellis, 2013; McClaurin, 2001; Spry, 2001), and ethics and "writing up" autoethnography (Conquergood, 1991, 2002, 2006; Durham, 2014; Ellis & Bochner, 1996; Goodall, 2000; Hurston, 1925; Jones, 1997; Schechner, 1985; Shange, 1977; Spry, 2011; Weems, 2003). Meeting the social justice call of qualitative research within this historic moment of inquiry (Denzin & Lincoln, 2008), autoethnography has provided space for qualitative researchers "writing to right" (Denzin & Lincoln, 2008; Hill, 2008). In doing so, autoethnography has also provided a space for qualitative researchers to speak on sensitive subjects and invite marginalized and silenced voices into contemporary conversations, policies, and research, thereby creating social change (Holman Jones, Adams, & Ellis, 2013).

The field of education remains reluctant to embrace auto/ethnography (Hughes, Pennington, & Makris, 2012). Evident in Sherick Hughes and Julie Pennington's (2017) *Autoethnography: Process, Product, and Possibility for Critical Social Research*, the headway of autoethnography into education is not without tension and epistemological quarrel. For instance, the current landscape of K-16 education is steeped in positivist assessments, including "causality-driven, evidence-based, traditional validity/reliability-based, replicable studies with interventions that can be scaled up" (p. 181), and provides particular difficulties for deploying autoethnographic research methods and findings. Hughes & Pennington admonish autoethnographers and particularly those within education to seriously consider these limitations and to grapple with how the goodness factor of autoethnography is measured and its true relevance to the field. Notably, researchers in the field employ auto/ethnography as a methodological approach to explore sociocultural identities and how they shape educational spaces (Alexander, 2006b; Brown, 2009; Nathan, 2005), approaches to curriculum and pedagogy (Hill, 2017; Hughes, Pennington, & Makris, 2012), and teacher reflexivity to improve educational experiences and outcomes (Hill, 2014b; Johnson, 2014; Ortner, 2005; Pennington, 2007; Romo, 2005). As the discipline wrestles with ways to broaden its scope and incorporate critically reflexive and culturally responsive theorizations of culture, the integration of auto/ethnography helps to address these aims, layers the documentation of social interactions between students and teachers, and frames teachers as agents of social justice and change. Simultaneously, there is a noted shift in the incorporation and exploration of the utility of auto/ethnography and a preservation of conventional methodological tools as gatekeepers within the discipline of education (Hughes & Pennington, 2017). Our approach has always been to highlight the importance of autoethnographic research as an intervention to many of the issues identified and taken up by critical educators and scholars both within and outside of K-16 schooling contexts. Understandably discipline specific, the conversations within education regarding the applicability and utility of autoethnography often limits its possibilities. Seeking to broaden these conversations, we return to foundational texts within the field and methodology of autoethnography.

In laying out a foundation for what auto/ethnography is and where it should be headed in education and other fields, Stacey Holman Jones, Tony Adams, and Carolyn Ellis (2013) identify several practices in *The Handbook of Autoethnography*. They include: "(1) disrupting norms of research practice and representation; (2) working from insider knowledge; (3) maneuvering through pain, confusion, anger and uncertainty and making life better; (4) breaking silence/(re)claiming voice and 'writing to right' (Bolen, 2012); and (5) making work accessible" (p. 32). These serve as core tenets of auto/ethnographic research. Robin Boylorn and Michael Orbe (2014) describe cultural-critical autoethnography as "the ways in which an intersectional approach to exploring the inextricable relationship between culture and communication (Orbe, 1998) and the influence of preexisting and potential relationships provides insights beyond that which is possible through frameworks" (pp. 18–19). In a more recent collection of autoethnographic works, Sandra L. Pensoneau-Conway, Tony Adams, and Derek Bolen (2017) provide exemplars of *doing* autoethnographic research. The exemplars included in this collection provide fresh insights into the past, present, and future of the methodology from a particularly interdisciplinary vantage. Both Boylorn and Orbe (2014) and Pensoneau-Conway, Adams, and Bolen (2017) provide important forays for seasoned researchers as well as newcomers to the methodology that build upon the critical foundations offered within the *Handbook of Autoethnography*. We extend the scholarship featured in the *Handbook* and *Critical Autoethnography* by forecasting a future of autoethnography that explicitly attends to collectivity, spirituality, collectivity, and the Black body.

MANIFESTING & AUTOETHNOGRAPHY: CHARTING
NEW DIRECTIONS IN THE FIELD

In a small classroom with wooden floors on a Saturday afternoon, approximately 20 people sat cypher-style. Seated in desks arranged in a circle, seven Black, diasporic women came together to talk about autoethnography, past, present, and future. Sacred space. Futuristic space. Were we hearing her correctly, she didn't identify her work as autoethnography? Why? On a panel full of Black feminist auto/ ethnographers? Her refusal, etymological and epistemological. She was refusing to be alone, to labor alone, to be acknowledged alone, seen as the sole creator of any of the knowledge she created. Community and the ancestors had to be present. She asked us, "Where does spirit live" in the work? With tear-stained eyes, we were moved. Moved to remember, moved to accept a challenge, moved to accept the call.

Before we can begin reflecting upon the moment that unfolded around our manifesto birthed at the 12th International Congress of Qualitative Inquiry, it is important to go back to the seventh iteration of the conference. Organized by Aisha Durham and chaired by Carolyn Randolph, the panel explored questions such as: What is Black feminist auto/ethnography, and what is the significance of the backslash? How can we deploy auto/ethnography to think about diaspora? Where is the space for community in the work? How does spirit live, move, and operate in the work? Autoethnography is a "spiritual act of political self-determination, of reclamation" (Durham, 2017, p. 23); being moved by spirit and sitting with the question of where it could be located within the work reiterated this knowing.

Nascent in our practice of autoethnography that was critical, collective, and performative, we, Hill L. Waters, sat in the audience as eager, invested, doctoral students. With commitments to communal and collective work that enhances Black diaspora lives, we came to soak up this opportunity to sit with women whose scholarship had not only indelibly touched us, but who had paved the way for us to do autoethnographic work. We showed up excited to learn from Black women. We showed up eager to learn how they articulated the work of auto/ethnography. We showed up hoping to see ourselves reflected back to us. What we found was a living genealogy of Black feminist auto/ethnography. The panel was made possible in part by Irma McClaurin's (2001) groundbreaking work in *Black Feminist Anthropology: Theory, Politics, Praxis, and Poetics*, which landscapes the terrain of Black feminism and anthropology. It brings to bear the work of

Black women in anthropology and provides exemplars of Black feminists conducting autoethnographic projects. *Black Feminist Anthropology* renders visible the labor of Black women in academe generally, and (auto) ethnography specifically.

We start here with this collective memory and recognition of a Black feminist genealogy of autoethnography, which fermented in our minds the possibilities of autoethnographic research, because manifesting the future is always about the palimpsest past/present/future possibilities existing simultaneously (Alexander, 2005). Inscribed forever on our bodies, we bear witness to the moment in which Waters penned the poem, Baptismal I:

6 women baptized me

Submerged me deep back into myself

Hovered round me

Laying hands

Casting out the demons tap-dancing on my medulla oblongata

My mother on the shore

Her mother to witness

I emerged anew

My funk still there

But mine

6 women baptized me

And said

Answer the call…

(D. Callier, personal communication, May 28, 2012)

The call, if we dared, was to take up auto/ethnography along with a Black feminist ethos that held community, interconnectivity, Black aesthetics, spirit, liberation, and emotionality as necessary pillars. In response to Cynthia Dillard's query on the place for community and spirit in autoethnographic work, Aisha Durham said,

…And I do think that when we say "I," especially within an African Diaspora and African centered, …the "I" is never this individualized; …it's everybody who came before us, and everybody before…So in

75

some ways if we want to think about a distinction in Black Feminist or Black Womanist auto/ethnography, I think it is that the "auto" itself is a collective "I" right, and so it/s not necessarily the "I" in the way that others may define auto/ethnography. (McClaurin, 2012)

Her reply illuminates Black feminist auto/ethnographic praxis as one which centers collectivity. Further, illustrating the pillars of this praxis were the tears shared by Maritza Quiñones, the spoken-word utterances of Mary Weems, the insistence of collective labor, spiritual grounding, and a communal utility of the method as expressed by Cynthia Dillard and Aisha Durham, as well as Robin Boylorn's insistence that Black feminist auto/ethnography is life-saving and Black-life-affirming. Collectively, we conjured community, and I/we speak. In that room, we wrestled with external constructions of the self-imposed on Black feminist communal thinking and writing. As we, two young scholar-artists eager to find our homes in academe, witnessed the poetic knowledge production occurring in the space, we began to answer the call of auto/ethnography.

Our collective practice parallels the centrality of ancestral and community accompaniment to methodology as laid out during the "Poetics, Politics, and Praxis of Producing Black Feminist and Womanist Auto/ethnography" panel during the 7th International Congress of Qualitative Inquiry. Our collective autoethnographic practice began the year before, but on that day in 2012, the call was more pronounced. Since that moment, we have continued to incorporate its beckoning within our collective practice, recognizing as did Dillard (2012) and Alexander (2005) that the spiritual is political and personal and necessary to our liberatory struggles and research practices. Moreover, our practice shifts autoethnography to an auto (self) that is never singular, never just the individual, but always insistently collective. What unfolds below is a continuation of that practice and an answer to the call to invoke autoethnography into the future – a future that holds room for our "funk" (Weems, personal communication, May 19, 2012), our tears (McClaurin, 2012), garbage men's kids (Alexander, 2000), resistance stories (Alexander, Moreira, & Kumar, 2012; Moreira & Diversi, 2010), family and southern, Black, rural women's resilience (Boylorn, 2013b), complex identities (Callier, 2012), vulnerability (Hill, 2014b, 2017), Blackness, and the reclamation of ourselves (Brown, 2009; Durham, 2003; Johnson, 2014; Richardson, 2013).

As a mode of emboldening sociocultural realities and structures and the personal, auto/ethnography has a responsibility to stretch and provide redress to the current United States cultural climate. With this societal moment marked by increased surveillance, harm, and death of Black and queer bodies (Aronson & Boveda, 2017; Callier, 2011, 2013, 2018; Cobb, 2014; Goodman & González, 2003; James, 2009; Johnson et al., 2017; J. King, 2014), devaluation of scholars of color and the labor of women of color, knowledge production and genius (Brown, Carducci, & Kuby, 2014; Brown, 2014; Gutierrez y Muhs et al., 2012; Jaschik, 2015), and the neoliberal impulses which continue to dismantle public goods and education in particular (Davies & Bansel, 2007), we considered/are still considering what tools might intervene and counteract a moment saturated in loss, blatant disregard for bodies Black, queer, or Blackqueer, bodies relegated to the fringes of citizenship and humanity. Performance and a close slow dance between auto/ethnography, education, and performance are our answers.

Equally so, autoethnographers must answer the call of autoethnography in this moment. It is our responsibility to consider the possibilities of autoethnographic labor in the future, its politics, possibilities, and praxis. Taking this seriously, we situate one future of auto/ethnography, as Black and queer as we are, as a collective practice that wrestles not with the idea of I/we as insider/outsider positionalities, but in regards to subjecthood, a practice that reorients our strategies of resistance, organizing, researching, and changing the world to dynamics of shared, collective decision-making and knowledge production (Brown, 2013). To put it another way, we explore how auto/ethnography can (continue to) persist in ways in which "the auto itself is collective" (Aisha Durham, personal communication, May 19, 2012).

What follows is our manifesto for the future of autoethnography. Manifestos have a history within political protests and organizing labor. Whether the Queer Nation Manifesto (1990) or the Combahee River Collective Statement (1977), manifestos draw upon a sense of collective visioning, survival, and freedom. At their core, they are architectures of critical thought and theory turned toward an eye of enacting a public praxis. They demand accountability from those co-conspirators who labor with and for the cause and from those who consciously and unconsciously perpetuate systems of domination and oppression. In her call to us, Stacy Holman Jones asked autoethnographers to join in this legacy, to come together as a community and make our collective motives known. What future(s) might we seek to birth collectively?

This is and was ritual. Call and response. Calling out to those within a community, awaiting their response to your presence, to your invitation, to the performance of love, accountability, and wholeness co-created in your coming together. Call and response is at home within Black cultural spaces and traditions, performing the calling out and responding to that calling. It is a co-leadership model of sharing time, space, resources, bodily presence, collective memory, self-determination, and a will to survive together, at the edge of each other's battles for a better tomorrow (Lorde, 1984, p. 123). Locating Black performance and ritual within Black freedom struggles and culture, hooks (1995b) offers two modes of Black performance: one ritualistic as a part of culture building, and the other manipulative out of necessity for survival in an oppressive world. As a vehicle for self-definition, performance was (and remains) one of the few autonomous spaces where Black people transgress boundaries meant to dehumanize their experiences. Also within performance, liberatory consciousness was learned, created, practiced, and passed down from generation to generation (hooks, 1995b; Johnson, 2006).

The ritual of call and response makes room and worlds. This worldmaking has been a collective means of maintaining doorways and connections to ancestors no longer here with us. Interrupting the voyeuristic consumption of Blackness, Black pain, suffering, and death, we enact rituals of remembrance. We enact call and response in our scholarship to invite into spaces – academic, performance, conference, and communal – ancestral Black, queer, and Blackqueer persons, and oblige those present to bear witness and respond to their experience as well as our storying of their lives. Performance autoethnography allows for a retelling of the Black body and death as "past presence" (Durham, 2017, p. 22). Through performance, our bodies, as time-traveling and time-containing vessels, bring forth our personal individual histories as well as collective histories endured by bodies Black, queer, or Blackqueer, like but not identical to ours. Moreover, aware that performance is ritual and functions as ritual, the process of doing and making rituals cultivates new knowledge. The act of knowing, then, is again rooted in a past presence. What has happened to the Blackqueer body? What is happening to the Blackqueer body? To my body? And how might that excavated knowledge create a different present? This is exemplified in Aisha Durham's (2017) (re)membering of the ritual of performance and narrative for herself in making collards with the living memories of her mothers.

For my black southern self, there is only past-presence. Forward-time and futurity feel like luxuries for folks whose dead are already remembered during parades, recited at elementary school plays, or reserved for national holydays. These timekeepers can hold hands while black ones are perpetually emptied but busily pantomiming the master. Narratives never allow us to speak – to us – or to the many other(ed) mothers who "make do" by making time to hand down across-ocean foodways and folk tales so we might be freed (up) to find ourselves – some time. (pp. 22–23)

Resembling Durham's Black girl-woman self-making and (re)membering making collards and the knowledge acquired and made in the process, we endeavored to make an embodied ritual. To *know* and *remember* is Incense Circle ritual where everyone present stands in a circle around a candle and shares the name(s) of someone or something they want us to know and remember (Brown, 2009). As scholars committed to taking what we have come to know with us, our knowing and remembering through manifesto meant an opportunity for Hill L. Waters to take stage and call attention to stakes informing our work as a collective specifically, and correspondingly, the work of qualitative research. To fill the stage with our Blackqueer bodies and narratives – historical, personal, collective, cultural – is to perform Blackness. Specifically, it was an opportunity to perform Blackness as a past-presence. Because our dead are seldom remembered, we needed moments to mourn, to remember, to celebrate, to call and respond as a chorus. To intentionally designate our breath in that moment to memorializing those bodies and beings rendered spectacles of death on the news is to know: (1) Black death is also a beginning, an opportunity, and (2) something happens (perhaps some justice) when folks are made to remember inconvenient truths. Equally, our deliberate placement of particularly Black and queer bodies on stage is to understand and work with spectacle.

This spectacle is a script, a script which Durham (2017) notes is something that rarely allows us to talk to one another. As a means of seeing, scripts rarely allow us to see each other "eye to eye," as Lorde (1984) so poignantly recalls. Autoethnography as an analytical tool works against these sociocultural scripts, often contrived as stereotypes, made to guilt and shame, or as performances of identity, authentic self, especially when read in and against the "overly determined space of social interactions" (Cox, 2015, p. 257). Aimee Cox (2015) notes that this is particularly true for "young Black women are always in the process of mediating the space between who they are and how they are seen, and between their theoretical rights as citizens and the reality of their exclusion from full recognition as citizens" (p. 258). Considering Cox (2015), we have aimed to actualize other performances of the self which might recognize and respond to such realities while simultaneously rejecting them. This was a part of the aim of our manifesto. Moreover, consistent with Cox's attention to the particularity of Black girls' lived experiences, we wanted to consider auto/ethnography informed by the lessons learned from our practice of working with Black girls and celebrating Black girlhood through SOLHOT and our own lived experiences. What possibilities could be realized for a methodology that drew its ethics from being in community with Black girls and built its epistemological foundations upon the kinesthetic and embodied knowledge of Black girlhood, "the representation, memories, and lived experiences of being and becoming in a body marked as youthful, Black, and female" (Brown, 2009, p. 1)?

Our thoughts on levitation as a particular vision for autoethnography builds upon Holman Jones, Adams, and Ellis' (2013) articulations of the purpose of autoethnography, while drawing upon Black girlhood, Black feminist practices of poetics, politics, and liberatory education. From their sonic sounds and digital archive, We Levitate provides important considerations for the field of auto/ethnography. They describe their project as "feeling ourselves beautiful through each other's voice, rhythm, and (heart) beats. Post heartbreak, music moves us through hurt and wisdom, to sing a new Black girl song" (We Levitate, 2017). The idea of "feeling ourselves beautiful through each other's voices" is similarly echoed in Nikky Finney's "Brown Girl Levitation," where she says, "I would lean hard into that high, elephant-lifting wind/with everything I had, carrying my girl mind & muscle/to the thing that I knew had been grandmother sent,/engineered, just for me."

Both Finney and We Levitate offer the idea of a gift and knowing, a particularity which is Black girlhood/womanhood and a shift in gaze in terms of how Black girls specifically and Black people broadly can be seen and known. Made in and through community, the gaze shifts; it is "grandmother sent" and we are "beautiful through each other's voices." This was our hope, that autoethnographies would manifest Black girlhood, and the practice of being in community with, loved by, seen by, and seeing Black girls would be held as central to the practice.

The script below testifies to the ephemeral nature of performance and the truth of the matter when Saldaña (2006) states, "You should have been there" (p. 1094). Said differently, "Performance may be theorized about, but the theory of the performance is imbedded in the performance itself, 'flaws' and all. The provocative question is not 'What theory created this performance?' but 'What theory is revealed through this performance?'" (Jones, 1997, p. 55). In our work of rendering visible complex narratives and visions of Blackness and Blackened autoethnographies, the manifesto below is a representation of the original performance, which was animated between our Black bodies upon a make-shift stage with autoethnographers in our community beholding and witnessing us.

What we offer here are the words we shared and stage directions, inclusive of music cues. We ask you to hold the weight of our layered text. Intentional and reflective of the liveliness of performance, the written text below is meant to be read and heard alongside music, visual images, our bodies, and Hill's dancing body in particular, which have all become flattened in this representation. Despite these absences, we ask you to journey with us through our five manifestations for the future of autoethnography: (i) levitation, (ii) collectivity, (iii) Black love/joy, (iv) pedagogy of affirmation, and (v) freedom. Each of these manifestations speak to our current historical moment and the challenge of Black feminist auto/ethnography as laid out in 2012.

WATERS: Hello. I am Durell M. Callier and this (*gesturing toward Dominique*) is Dominique, and when our powers combine, we are Hill L. Waters. I'm Waters and this is Hill. Hill L. Waters (HLW) is our queer practice to answer the call of auto/ethnography through performance, collective inquiry, and art. Welcome to our performative offering of the things we wish our work as collaborative auto/ethnographers to manifest. Sit back, enjoy, and…

Cue music: HomeGirlsHandMadeGrenades, "just don't never give up on love" //mix 1 plays throughout entire performance

I: Levitation
Movement: Hill

As music fades up, Hill makes extended eye contact with those in the room. She moves atop a wobbly table, goes into the audience, and gives a head nod to a sistascholar in the room. Hill stops dancing as the music fades but continues playing softly in the background.

II: Collectivity

HILL: who are you loving
WATERS: how are you loving
HILL: that is the question
WATERS: who are you healing
HILL: how are you healing
WATERS: that is the work
HILL: loving

WATERS: healing
HILL L. WATERS: the work

III: (Black) Love/Joy

WATERS: the night Mike Brown was indicted
I wanted to find the sweeeeeeetest chocolate boy
hold him close
and whisper sweet somethings in his ear
all night till morning

tonight all the chocolate boys are hugging their chocolate babies a little closer
counting the blessings of breath
heart beats
and small sweet hands
watching tenderly
as they whisper (to them)

whispering revolt, revolt, reeeeevoltttttt

IV: Pedagogy of Affirmation[1]

Waters: a la Toni Cade Bambara

HILL L. WATERS (*at will*): "Of course we know how to walk on the water, of course we know how to fly; fear of sinking, though, sometimes keeps us from the first crucial move, then too, the terrible educations you liable to get is designed to make you destruct the journey entire."

V: Freedom

WATERS: Freedom to me is…
like Nina said, "no fear"…
when walking while Black
while Black and queer
while being me period
doesn't come with the risk of making (or not making) national news,
joining a long list of others whose lives were taken too soon

Hill enters stage, begins to move at will

Freedom to me is…
ephemeral
a journey

dying a li'l to come back better
is here, now
like Bree Newsome
the future we deserve
a longing
work and responsibility

no debt
being able to read
add fractions
have your native tongue be honored
and your home valued in schools even if it is broken or different
dressing how one feels and it being okay
knowing the consequences and doing it anyway
knowing where you came from and where you want to go

choosing to be tied up but not imprisoned by another

Freedom to me is…

a lot of nots
like not…
(*improv other nots*)

like not having to think twice about kissing my lover in public

holding his hand in the bar
trying to gauge how safe here is

like not
like not
like not
like not

HILL L. WATERS: Like freedom, a love in praxis
music fades down and out at 10:52

REFLECTION QUESTIONS & INTERACTIVE EXERCISE

General Questions

- What are the benefits of examining gaze in community?
- How is love centered within your research practice?

For Educators

• What are the primary ingredients of your pedagogy?
• How, if at all, is love centered within your teaching and pedagogy?

Bodies on the Line

This activity has two levels on which you can engage, with the second being experiential and therefore a vulnerable undertaking.

Level One: Think back to a time that you felt your body was exposed, somehow on display, and (1) write about the moment. When was it? Where were you? What happened? How did you respond? (2) Using your reflection and memory of the event, write down the different angles of gaze onto your body. In other words, make note of who was looking at you. (3) Describe a feeling and/or reaction to each gaze. Lastly, (4) think through and/or write out what about this event made you feel your body was exposed.

Level Two: Create a list of places, events, and acts that would place your body on the line. (1) Review and narrow the list by crossing out actions that would put you in immediate physical, psychological, and/or emotional harm. (2) Look at the list and choose something that would create some discomfort. (3) Do that thing. (4) Afterward, reflect on the experience by writing down your immediate reactions. (5) Consider how gaze operated in the event, including the different angles of gaze onto your body. In other words, make note of who was looking at you. (6) What did this event reveal to you about gaze?

NOTE

[1]   Taken from Toni Cade Bambara's (1996) "The Education of a Storyteller," the quote (p. 255) during this moment in the performance was performed round-robin and at will by Hill and Waters. It was spoken aloud, verbatim by each performer once, with each subsequent round deployed in a nonsensical fashion, as poet and legal scholar M. NourbeSe Philip utilizes in *Zong!* (2008). As we deploy this nonsense-making of the "terrible educations" Black and queer folks are liable to receive, we sought a way in our utterances, devolved language, broken words, syllables, letters, sounds, and silences to tell stories that resist being told. When the bodies lay waste and disappeared, consumed by the terrible educations, how do you tell a story of life or life in death if you cannot retrieve the bones (Philip, 2008)? In breaking the text, we also break scriptocentric forms of knowing, and transgress those oppressive regimes of knowledge which police, devalue, and destroy Black, queer ways of knowing, being, and thriving – a pedagogy of affirmation and hope.

5. WHEN WE LOOK AT EACH OTHER

An Auto/Ethnography of Togetherness

> As Black people, if there is one thing we can learn from the 60s, it is how infinitely complex any move for liberation must be. For we must move against not only those forces which dehumanize us from the outside, but also again those oppressive values which we have been forced to take into ourselves. (Lorde, 1984, p. 135)

I often dream. Part premonition, part admonishment from spirit. Always clarity. On the day in which we began this chapter, I was roused from my sleep by a dream.

In my dream, there was a Black woman academic. her physique and command of the space translated to a Stormesque, Nell Irvin Painter, sharp, sister god. a sista docta friend of mine, Shotgun Annie, asked this Black woman, "how do you learn how to undo what has been done to you?" her answer, "god is a form" and it's figuring out how to be the form of the god(s) you know…not the gods you were taught in order to be seen as middle class and respectable…not the gods who take you away from your own kin and skin…the scene in my mind, turned adjacent to another Black woman who was also in the audience, listening in on this *how to survive (the academy): everything you need to know and already knew (but pretend not to)* lesson. i could only make out her side profile at first, and as i came closer to her visage, i saw the tears welling in her eyes. then the one that cascaded down her cheek. i think the tears were a mixture of pride and something else that struck a nerve. she was proud of her child who went off to achieve something, something that i think was like graduating from college but her child had done so in a way that had forsaken her…

Since the dream, I have listened to Tank and the Bangas describe their own struggles with staying in college, lyrically resolving, "I must go, I must leave…the concept of school seem so secure, but it ain't." This morning, I was also made to recall a portion of Lorraine Hansberry's 1959 speech, "The Negro Writer and His Roots: Towards a New Romanticism," given at a major Black writer's conference in which she states,

> I wish to live because life has within it that which is good, that which is beautiful, and that which is love. Therefore, since I have known all of

© KONINKLIJKE BRILL NV, LEIDEN, 2019 | DOI:10.1163/9789004392243_006

these things, I have found them to be reason enough and – I wish to live. Moreover, because this is so, I wish others to live for generations and generations and generations and generations. (Hansberry, 1981, p. 12)

I came across Audre Lorde's *The Cancer Journals* (1997b). I mention all of these, the dream, Tank, Sweet Lorraine, and Audre Lorde because of their synchronicity. The clarity of my dream was manifested over several reminders and interactions on the day in which we – Hill L. Waters – are writing about not experiencing the academy alone. The reasons, our survival. The blueprints, ancestral. What we are clear about is that the practice of being in community[1] and doing collective, accountable work is what makes our work as auto/ethnographers possible. Refusing to be (a)lone autoethnographer grounds us in ways that allow us to acknowledge spirit (Dillard, 2012; McClaurin, 2012), disrupt boundaries and ways of being/doing qualitative research in education (Brown et al., 2014), and actualize decolonial praxes rooted in Black feminist knowledge and practices (Alexander, 2005; Gumbs, 2016; McClaurin, 2001).

In this chapter, we explore the idea of refusal and the methodological approach to autoethnography that emerges from our collective praxis. Through narrative reflection rooted in our intentional refusal to be the lone (auto)ethnographer and refusing to do academe alone, we provide a framework for collective auto/ethnography and being/doing collective auto/ethnography. We first provide a skeletal landscape of ethnography as related to the "lone ethnographer" approach and auto/ethnography. Next, we situate our work within/out this landscape, while also tying it to the work of Black community organizing. Employing an alternative frame of love between Black men and women, a queer love practice, we offer love letters, written unknowingly with each other in mind during Black Girl Genius Week (BGGW),[2] a week-long event dedicated to being with, making space for, and celebrating Black girls and Black girlhood. The final section ends with a poetic closing and reflection on the origins and fruits of our collective labor together as/in autoethnographers.

SEARCHING FOR COLLECTIVITY IN AUTO/ETHNOGRAPHY

As a palimpsest, the period of qualitative research we are currently writing, living, and researching through is still marked by previous periods (Denzin & Lincoln, 2008). Reaching beyond the conversation in Chapter 4 around defining moments in autoethnography, here we contextualize the history within the larger field of qualitative research. One such period is the classic period in qualitative research, in which traditional ethnography was performed, where the lone ethnographer, who studied culture over there, objectively, was privileged (Denzin & Lincoln, 2002; Rosaldo, 1989). A precursor to autoethnography, this form of ethnographic research – classical ethnography – was often complicit in imperialism, devoid of cultural relativism, unaware of the researcher's positionality, culture, and bias, and believed in monumentalism and the timelessness of the study – the ability to create a museum-like and unchangeable representation of the culture (Denzin & Lincoln, 2002; Rosaldo, 1989). In noting the turn to the *creative analytic practice* in qualitative research writing, Richardson (2000) identifies how qualitative researchers shifted their writing to more reflexive and narrative forms. Autoethnography was one of these forms and shifts.

It is important to note that there are other ways to see ethnography and autoethnography. For instance, Deck (1990) highlights the ways that cultural explication and personal narrative intertwine in anthropologist Zora Neal Hurston's ethnographic research in the southern United States and the Caribbean. Hurston's 1942 memoir, *Dust Tracks on a Road*, based on her ethnographic research and experiences in observing and understanding the folk tales, songs, and religious rituals of Black people in the United States and the Caribbean, is often labeled as an autobiographical text. However, as Deck (1990) demonstrates, it is important to understand Hurston's ethnographic research within a cross-cultural and historic context which,

> includes texts by Americans from other ethnic groups as well as a few of the personal narratives of Western-educated Africans. The Chinese-American Maxine Hong Kingston's *The Woman Warrior*, the Native American Beverly Hungry Wolf's *The Ways of My Grandmothers*, Kenyans (Kikuyu) Jomo Kenyatta's *Facing Mount Kenya* and Charity Waciuma's *Daughter of Mumbi*, Guinean (Malinke) Camara Laye's *L'Enfant noir*, and the South African (Xhosa) Noni Jabavu's *Drawn in Colour* and *The Ochre People* demonstrate the same dialogic, polyphonic structure as does Hurston's *Dust Tracks on a Road*. (p. 2)

Hurston's work as autobiographical ethnography stands as a precursor to the now-accepted term and methodology of autoethnography. Further, as Jones (1997) demonstrates, the autobiography of "marginalized peoples often serves as a collective biography, giving name to the experiences of many through the experiences of one" (p. 51). In this way, Hurston's work – part autobiography, part ethnography – centers the ethos of autoethnography. Her work and the work of those previously mentioned (e.g., Noni Jabavu)

87

demonstrate this ethos through the usage of voice, reflexivity, narration, and analyses that center the situatedness of self with others in social contexts (Brown, 2009; Deck, 1990; Spry, 2001).

In addition to understanding the complicated history of autobiography, memoir, ethnography, reflexive relationships within ethnography, and how those shape autoethnography and collaboration with field participants, it is also important to understand the multiple names for collaborative forms of autoethnography. We include here a non-exhaustive list of autoethnographic research and writing that moves beyond the individual self, thus seeking to investigate the self and collective in relationship to various phenomena. Such examples include autoethnography (Brown, 2009), Black feminist auto/ethnography (Durham, 2014; McClaurin, 2001, 2012), critical auto/ethnography (Boylorn & Orbe, 2014), performance ethnography (Jones, 1997), performative autoethnography (Spry, 2016), critical (auto)ethnography (Diversi & Moreira, 2009), tri-autoethnography (Alexander, Moreira, & Kumar, 2012), collaborative writing (Weems, Callier, & Boylorn, 2014), collaborative autoethnography (Gale et al., 2013; Wyatt et al., 2011), duo ethnography (Norris, Sawyer, & Lund, 2016), collective auto/ethnography (Callier, Hill, & Waters, 2017b), and autobiographical ethnography (Deck, 1990). What each of these have in common is a centering of the self with others in social contexts to reveal the inner workings of culture. Here, we highlight the array of ways to do autoethnography, with and in community. Teasing out some of the examples above, Brown's (2009) autoethnographic research in *Black Girlhood Celebration* is based on her ethnographic research with Black girls as she wrestles with the simultaneity of being a Black woman/girl working with and for Black women/girls. Other ways of doing autoethnographic research and writing highlight the co-exploration of phenomena in concert with other individuals. These include but are not limited to tri-autoethnography (Alexander, Moreira, & Kumar, 2012) and collaborative autoethnography (Gale et al., 2013). Lastly, as Aisha Durham states, Black feminist auto/ethnography situates itself within an African Diaspora and African-centered way of knowing, in which the "auto" itself is a collective "I" (McClaurin, 2012).

There are many names for the work, and with whom and how autoethnographers collaborate and/or labor collectively reveals facets of our culture. As demonstrated above, sometimes autoethnographers collaborate with other people within and beyond researchers, home communities, affinity groups, or with/in community. Sometimes the collaboration is with spirit. Other times, autoethnographers operate from an ontological frame that recognizes that the "I" is never a sole individual alone in the world. Pertinent to understanding the plethora of approaches to autoethnography and the role of collaboration is how such intentions permeate the research process (e.g., research design, analysis, and representation of data). Within our research, the permeation of collaboration has shown up as collectivity. Underscoring our own epistemological values and political commitments in the research, we have chosen to write together as an "I" plural.

MORE THAN COLLABORATION, WE LOVE EACH OTHER: COMING TO COLLECTIVE AUTO/ETHNOGRAPHY

In a room of the Champaign, Illinois public library, with anywhere between 35 and 50 folk in attendance, young and seasoned alike, Saving Our Lives Hear Our Truths (SOLHOT) is in session. It's the inaugural Black Girl Genius Week, a week-long public and sacred intergenerational practice of bringing together artists, scholars, and healers to deepen the work of Black girlhood celebration. Today, we are writing a letter to our best friend. Our best friends, unknowingly, are in the room.

We begin to write.

Dear Durell,

Thank you. For just being you. I know in the beginning i couldn't tell if you were being my friend or being nice but I know. I know you are loving, beautiful, and full of sooo much goodness. You are love. Your smile is so necessary to this world and I couldn't imagine not seeing it and not having it light up dark rooms.

Over the years there has been so much transition, misunderstanding, and loss. People have left and you have stayed. People have thrown shade and you have come closer. I had no idea i'd gain a brother a husband a best friend in you. But that's the beauty of it, this thing called love. All it takes is showin up and you have shown up over and over again.

You teach me what it means to dig deep and see beyond my projections of how things are to ask questions, to ask for more, and to wait for those requests to show. And again, you show up. I could've never asked for a being like you. I could've put together a list of attributes and qualities in a friend. And yet I got everything I needed. I got you.

The thing about it is that you grow with me. I learn from you. I hear you and you hear me. I see you and you me. I haven't had many besties in my life because I take that shit seriously. Without a doubt, you have made your way into my heart, my family, my future.

You are loved handsome,

Dominique

11.8.2014

***

I don't think that you know i consider you like a best friend. But that night, I told you real shit about myself, shared parts of me that nobody else knew and still very few know. That was it. No more lies. You hugged me without hesitation and your first words to me were, "I am here and I still going to be here." We hugged, we cried together, and took deep breaths in. I am sooooo grateful that you are a part of my life. I watch you constantly, studying your passion, your drive, your persistence, your ability to overcome, your commitment to being your best self, always aiming to be better. You inspire me in ways you don't even know. I don't count many friends as best friends. I haven't had many if any at all. What I do know is that if you're really a friend of mine, then you're family to me (AND that's big shit). I resist labels, we both do, but the work of our friendship is what matters most to me. Thank you for loving me unconditionally, for putting up with my indecisiveness, my unwillingness to yield at times, my cancerian narcissism. Thank you for teaching me to love myself, for helping me to live more in my own body. Thank you for the drunk nights, the warm meals, the laughs, the hugs, the opening yourself and family to me.

More grateful than you'll ever know

11/8/14

After this sharing moment, after implicit references to our friendship and his letter, I disclose that I wrote my letter to him and consider him family. Unknowingly, we wrote these letters to each other on November 8, 2014. Unknowingly, when the floor opened for sharing, Waters read his letter aloud. With a recently emptied bladder, Hill entered the room only to catch the tail end of letter, with no idea to whom Waters' letter was dedicated. The conversations unfolding here, in the preceding love letters and poems above, are private, intimate whispers, shared first with self, interrogated in the self, then shared in secret with another. They are glimpses into the underbelly of Black intracultural conflict, plausible justifications for why we would not collaborate, reasonable excuses for why time toward collectivity could be used in other ways, and what grounds our specific collective. These conversations made public serve as pronouncement of our value for a clean house.

Being in conversation *with* one another entails another kind of work, of being *with/in* conversation, deeply, intimately, vulnerably, and truthfully with ourselves (Alexander, 2005; Bambara, 1969; Gordon, 2005). Furthermore, the questions posed within these conversations take up other larger issues related to our conceptualization of what is revolution(ary), freedom, and the work necessary to create and sustain revolution/change: collectivity. As illustrated throughout this chapter, it is our belief that revolution, beginning with a new way of seeing (Black) bodies, is an individual and collective project.

Beginning in 2010 as part of a graduate class project, we began reflecting together on the possibility, responsibility, and goals of a collective. During this time of considering and digging into the muck of community, specifically between Black men and women, when browsing historical documents and contemporary cultural archives left us disappointed but not surprised, we recognized the dearth of collectivity between Black men and women. Questions swirled: Do Black men and women only work together for "Black causes," causes absent of feminist ideals? What (should) sit(s) at the root of Black men and women collective work? At the time, we did not deem our awareness novel, but rather, recognized it as a doorway. What could we dare manifest by creating a collective between a Black man and woman? In the absence of sex as a communing act, what would be our glue? Love. An L., cleaving together Hill's paternal and Callier's matrilineal sides, resting at the center of our chosen name, Hill L. Waters.

At the time of this initial reflection, however, there was no name, only a commitment to doing work that extended "what we now know and how we know it" (Brown, 2009, 2013). Labor in the name of self-saving (Garner, 2011), labor that is back-breaking, that leaves aches all over your body and spirit, must be done in collectivity and SOLHOT. Ruth Nicole Brown taught us that. Part of this process entailed sifting through the mud of historical and cultural mythologies and narratives of Black women and men, which place us at odds. It also involved talking with each other about our thoughts on and experiences with interacting with the opposite sex, as well as our hopes for the future of the Black community. We transcribed these recorded discussions and converted our dense and heavy dialogue to a series of poems titled, *We Say We Love Each Other*. To close, we offer an excerpt from this series:

We Say We Love Each Other

WATERS & HILL: Love is

HILL: I love you

WATERS: I love you

HILL: Some simply wanting to

Gain freedom

See each other, clearly,

WATERS: visibly

WATERS & HILL: as we really are

WATERS: Listen intently with our bodies

Continue to love in spite of the lack I feel in your presence

WATERS & HILL: love is

HILL: the unknown

WATERS: where we think we headed

HILL: something

disconnected

WATERS & HILL:

love IS

ourselves

Co-authored

A love poem

to each other

(Love, Funk, & Other Thangs, 2012)

When we look at each other, we see a "love poem." Refusing to do auto/ ethnography alone has recalibrated our sight, to see Blackness, queerness, and Black femininity more complexly. For us, shifting the gaze has also been about the methodological approach to doing this type of research. We place front-and-center knowing through our bodies, our bodies' connectedness, their rub, and corresponding to remake our individual ones and create a new singular but not individual one. In doing this work, as friends who constructed a collective from an ethical and communal imperative, we have also manifested to one another a promise of survival[3] (Gumbs, 2012).

REFLECTION QUESTIONS

General Questions

- How do you relate to the concepts collaboration and collectivity?
- When was the last time you collaborated to bring an idea, event, or action to fruition? What was the outcome?
- What do you consider to be the benefits and responsibility of examining gaze in community?

For Educators

- What qualities do you consider necessary to establishing connection, particularly with potential collaborators?
- What risks, real and imagined, inform your approach to working with youth, particularly Black youth?

NOTES

[1] See Saving Our Lives Hear Our Truths (SOLHOT) and Eternal Summer of the Black Feminist Mind.

[2] Black Girl Genius Week was a week-long celebration originally held in 2014. The event was initially staged by SOLHOT homegirls at the University of Illinois at Urbana-Champaign, and included a variety of artists, scholars, organizers, and cultural workers who celebrated and worked with and for Black girls.

[3] Here we are referencing Alexis Pauline Gumbs' (2012) notion of survival: "Survival references our living in the context of what we have overcome. Survival is life after disaster, life in honor of our ancestors, despite the genocidal forces worked against them specifically so we would not exist. I love the word survival because it places my life in the context of those who I love, who are called dead, but survive through my breathing, my presence, and my remembering. They survive in my stubborn use of the word survival unmodified. My survival, my life resplendent, with the energy of my ancestors, is enough."

SHIFTING SOCIOCULTURAL GAZES

Toward Seeing Blackness Anew

I am black alive and looking back at you. (Jordan, 1969, p. 31)

Who Look at Me (Jordan, 1969) is the book-length poem that has not only inspired this book but has been the sinew weaving each chapter together. Here, we want to revisit the significance of the work and how it has been integral to our labor, as well as what possibilities it imagines with our research practices and in our efforts toward fighting and dismantling systems of domination. In the 1960s, Jordan's commitment to freedom was resolute and steadfast. This was evidenced in her participation in the fight for civil rights in Southern states; she wrote for newspapers, visited Black communities heavily impacted by racism, segregation, and racialized violence, joined the freedom rides, and worked closely with Fannie Lou Hamer (Kinloch, 2006). It was also during this time that Jordan wrote *Who Look at Me*, depicting the "strength and beauty of black and interracial lives, experiences, and identities by telling the stories of twenty-seven colorful paintings that portray aspects of black life" (Kinloch, 2006, p. 38). The book is a tripartite exemplar and call to action in how it attests to collective action and love, provides a methodologically rich, layered text of meaning, and engages gaze, or as Kinloch (2006) states, "the contemptuous stares of white people" (p. 39).

Attesting to collective action and love, *Who Look at Me* demonstrates what it means to intentionally love Black people. It was Jordan's love for her friend Langston Hughes that pushed her to pick up his mantle and continue to work on *Who Look at Me* after his death. Moreover, the project is encouraged by several friends and the times, by being in relationship to a community, and by being invested in collective care and self-determination. Locating collectivity in the singular and the singular within a collective, "me" and "I" are used amongst "we" and "a people" throughout the book-length poem. Jordan's willingness to continue the labor of a comrade and her attention to I-plural reveal her boundless love of, for, and with Black people. This sense of collectivity also demonstrates Jordan's vision, which saw her as

© KONINKLIJKE BRILL NV, LEIDEN, 2019 | DOI:10.1163/9789004392243_007

interconnected and saw us as interdependent upon one another – a radical, Black love (Alexander, 2005; Johnson et al., 2017). Such radical love was also evident in her words as she worked to shift how Blackness and Black people are viewed. This is illustrated pointedly in how the book ends:

> I trust you will remember how we tried to love
> above the pocket deadly need to please
> and how so many of us died there
> on our knees.
>
> Who see the roof and corners of my pride
> to be (as you are) free?

WHO LOOK AT ME? (Jordan, 1969, pp. 90–91)

Attending to gaze, although Jordan indicts a white supremacist gaze, her view, her seeing is one which privileges seeing Black. On each page, Jordan rhetorically asks "who look" and "who see," offering up a lens of what Black people see and make of themselves in their own likeness. As Kinloch describes, Jordan seeks to "question the complexities of humanity, the nature of differences, and the unfairness of stereotypes" (Kinloch, 2006, p. 39). Read(er)s are confronted with a Black world and Black worldmaking – this is the gaze privileged in the text. It is how she asks each of us to see Black people and Blackness.

A methodologically rich text, *Who Look at Me* demonstrates the possibilities of rooted analysis and knowledge produced in the Black cultural milieu. How do we demonstrate our love of Blackness in our teaching and research? Jordan provides a blueprint. She answers as a directive cue for us to consider, "I am black alive and looking back at you" (Jordan, 1969, p. 31). To be Black, alive, and looking back is to be known to yourself and to others because you said so, as a subject rather than an object. Speaking as a subject, a human, somebody, Jordan demonstrates this subject positionality throughout the book as the poem produces Black humanity alongside the striking visual images of Black people, by Black artists, often peering back at the read(er)s. The methodological innovation of the text is two-fold and has been our guide throughout this book. On the one hand, Jordan demonstrates the possibilities of intertextual analysis and rendering. Bringing together visual art and poetry, we are challenged as read(er)s to hold the weight of both and to consider what meaning, theory, and knowledge can be made about life, about Blackness, and in service to Black people via art. This play on the possibility of different forms of knowledge being able to be produced beyond scriptocentric forms is important as we continue to consider how epistemology and methodological rigor, validity, and acceptance often hinge upon positivist paradigms (Brown, Carducci, & Kuby, 2014). After all, Jordan is a poet and knows that poetry, good poetry, must be read aloud (Mueller & The Poetry for the People Blueprint Collective, 1995).

Additionally, the fact that *Who Look at Me* is a book-length poem for children should not be lost. Reading this text aloud, interacting with the pictures, possibly in an intergenerational scene of a younger child being read to or reading to someone older was her intention. The episteme of this text is not rooted in its scriptocentric form, but in an embodied and performative nature, between bodies, voices, gazes, affect, touch, familial and familiar affinity.

On the other hand, Jordan's text provides a methodology that centers a Black epistemology, or as Dillard and Okpalaoka (2011) assert, an Endarkened Feminist Epistemology. In the face of perpetually recorded and viralized Black death, it is imperative that the methodologies utilized to generate knowledge for and with Black people do so on fertile Black grounds.

Mirroring Jordan's methodological interventions, her work with engaging gaze, and her enactment of collective action and love, we have offered this book with the same spirit and aims. We turned our gaze to look specifically at education, inclusive of how we teach, research, write analyses, disseminate research, and allow embodied knowledge to guide our pedagogy. Guided by Jordan's methodological query, "I am black alive and looking back at you," we question how our methodologies might change if we saw Black people as subjects and not objects – alive and human. What questions would we ask differently, how would we approach our research differently if we knew that the community in which we drew our knowledge from would look back at it and would look back at us?

BLACK SCENES/SEEN BLACK[1]

[b]ell hooks writes, "Teaching is a performative act. And it is that aspect of our work that offers the space for change, invention, spontaneous shifts that can serve as a catalyst drawing out the unique elements in each classroom" (1994, p. 11). We posit so too is gaze. Gaze functions as a vessel for mitigating relationships between bodies and other bodies, bodies and spaces, and persons and other persons. To underestimate or disregard the role of gaze in teaching and the educational processes is to miss opportunities of transformation, imagination, and critique. [h]ooks continues insisting that teaching situated as a performative act "calls everyone to become more and more engaged, to become active participants in learning" (p. 11). Inclusive of hooks' framing

of performance, we endeavor that through this text, you, read(er)s and gazers, are coming to see the value of performance to the educational enterprise and specifically to seeing the dimensionality of Blackness and queerness. Speaking specifically about performance as an instrument for recognizing Black girls' humanity, Brown (2013) suggests, "As a radical method, performance challenges disciplinary codes, thereby elevating the more emancipatory elements and affective impulses of social phenomena vital to critical thought, social justice organizing" (p. 26). Both Brown and hooks assert that there is something material, practical, and distinct about performance in relationship to sociocultural understandings and imaginings. Our deployment of performance in educational spaces, research, and now in this book afford a textured rendering of the interplay of Blackness, queerness, and context.

So, then, why performance and autoethnography in education now? Audre Lorde insists that we need different tools to both rehabilitate and make a new house. In her seminal essay on the master's tools, Lorde asks and answers. "What does it mean when the tools of a racist patriarchy are used to examine the fruits of that same patriarchy? It means that only the most narrow perimeters of change are possible and allowable" (Lorde, 1984, p. 111). Translating this question into education, what does it mean when the conventional tools used in education successfully disappear, hypervisibilize, and estrange particular individuals based on the bodies they inhabit? When these same tools are used to examine its fruits, what happens? It means that only those that sprout, grow, and come to be seen as fruits will be considered, that the boundaries of what constitutes fruit and not fruit will be confined to the master's tools. Below, we offer three scenes that embolden a sociocultural imaginary that situates Blackness as an underestimated, potential-filled, and over-surveilled site. Equally, these moments ask that we all cast a wider net (Jones, 2005) of what constitutes gaze and Blackness, and what education (should) have to say and do to create new scenes of possibility.

Scene 1: "With All Due Respect, what Would a Developing, Farming Country Have to Offer the Rest of us?"[2]

It is opening weekend of the blockbuster, critically acclaimed Marvel Cinematic Universe film, *Black Panther*. I am sitting still, basking in what I have just witnessed, waiting for any other end-credit scenes. Being somewhat akin to the sneak peek possibility that accompanies patience, I wait. The final scene unfolds, in which T'Challa, Okoye, Ayo, and Nakia are speaking at a United Nations meeting. This is significant for several reasons – T'Challa's father, T'Chaka, attended a similar meeting that ultimately led to his death, and T'Challa's speech opens the previously hidden and closed borders of Wakanda, the fictional African nation in Marvel Comics. It is a land that has managed to maintain Black ownership, rulership, and autonomy. A non-colonized people, Wakandans have developed the otherworldly sound- and energy-absorbing element known as vibranium into technological advancements unknown to the "developed" world. Wakanda has developed separately from colonized time and space into one of the most technologically advanced societies and geopolitical nations. The rest of the world has no idea that Wakanda is anything but an impoverished farming community.

T'Challa's announcement is interrupted by murmurs, looks of bewilderment, and held laughter. One of the representatives asks, "With all due respect, what would a developing, farming country have to offer the rest of us?"[3] The "us" in his statement implies the "developed world," the colonizers (and colonized), the technologically advanced, the non-Black, non-farm workers of the world. The general assumption is that these people couldn't possibly have anything to offer the rest of the world, or at the very least, they don't have as much to offer as other people and places might. I have lived in Wakanda all my life. That's the sort of world Black folks in Baltimore made. Growing up in a mostly Black city and public school system, I knew Black principals, women and men, working alongside Black janitors. We learned about apartheid and watched the election of South Africa's first democratically elected president, Nelson Rolihlahla Mandela. I was afforded the opportunity to celebrate Black History Month every year and experienced a curriculum which did not relegate Blackness to slavery and all the bad things ever done to us. Blackness and Black people were celebrated. I grew up knowing that we as Black people had offered and still continue to offer something valuable to the world, even if the world didn't know it. Growing up in Wakanda is complicated, as is actualizing Wakanda in any real sense in our educational contexts and practices. Just because I knew the possibilities of a world which sought to be decolonized didn't mean that I was free from the impacts of the colonial constructs of my possibilities, Black people, and our communities.

Juxtaposing the previous memories of terrible educations in Chapter 1 to our contemporary pop culture moment, it is important to note the way in which our fields of vision assume who has value. The reality unbeknownst to the fictional UN representative is that the Wakandans – Black people – have a great deal to offer the world. Similarly, within our pedagogical practices, critical education scholars have advocated that we shift how we understand the difficulties students from marginalized backgrounds encounter when coming into contact with schools. Chris Emdin's (2011) critique of science education is particularly poignant here, as he notes that we sometimes adopt notions that urban youth hold anti-science and anti-school mindsets, missing "that everyone is scientifically minded and that it is the environments' (school and society's) ineffectiveness in fostering the inherent interest that disfigures urban Black youth's passion for the sciences" (p. 284). It is not only their interest that we disfigure with regards to the sciences, but them as well. Throughout this book we have posed the question back to the world, instead of what could Wakanda possibly offer us, we have asked what have we missed by assuming that Wakanda is only a developing nation, its people only farmers, people without a rich history, heritage, and immense capacity to change the world should they choose and be nurtured to do so. Even if Wakanda was "only" a developing, farming country, worth and value and how we see worth should not be predicated upon technological advancements, modernity, and capitalist gains/capacity.

Scene 2: "Look, in the Sky! It's a Plane! It's a Bird! It's a Frog! [...] it's Just Little Ol' Me, Underdog!"[4]

As a child of the 90s, raised in part by my uncle, I watched a lot of reruns. One of the VHS tapes he owned, which I watched religiously, included the cartoon *Underdog*.[5] The bumbling superhero, shoeshine canine by occupation, possesses superhero strength, speed, endurance, and flight whenever "danger nears." A childhood favorite, I recall how Underdog was often mistaken for something or someone else. Before dashing upon any scene to save the day, he was often seen as first a plane, then maybe a bird, even a frog, and lastly as the beloved hero. He was often called into action by his darling girlfriend and TV reporter, Sweet Polly Purebred, who was always glad to see him.

In this universe, Underdog is rarely seen as both Underdog and Shoeshine Boy – he's always one or the other, but not both. Although this dichotomy is a typical hero/alter ego split, I want to return to the misrecognition of the hero in my childhood cartoons. This sort of misrecognition stages another scene for Black people: neither our physical bodies, our alter egos – the mask that "grins and lies"[6] – nor the heroine of any story ever recognizes us as gifts. Instead, our bodies become weaponized, and what is seen of us publicly stages the scene of injury and tragedy. Is it a cell phone or a gun?[7] A wallet or a gun?[8] A shower head or a gun?[9] A comb or a gun? A child holding a toy or a gun?[10] Were those hands or a gun? Guns or empty hands? Were those hands up or did they resist arrest? Did she lynch herself?[11] Did he shoot himself, handcuffed in the back seat of the police vehicle?[12] Did he sever his own spine, shackled in the back of their paddy wagon?[13] Were they simply travelers, lost and in need of a good Samaritan?[14] Do running Black men resemble targets on a range?[15] Did her too-smart mouth morph into an aiming mark?[16] Is sovereignty only respected on a federal wildlife refuge in Oregon but not in an apartment in Baltimore County?[17] Is he a child or an adult? Is she a child or an adult? Are they/we ever seen as children?[18]

Underdog is such a befitting name because of how often we as viewers are made to witness assumptions about who Underdog is in real life and what he is capable of doing. Underdog's mistaken identity is also befitting here, as we find ourselves embroiled in the heightened, recorded, and viralized dissemination of Black people being harmed and/or killed by police officers and vigilantes alike. Something assumed to be held by the Black person (in their hands, on their bodies, or their bodies in and of themselves) are too immediately assumed to be a fatally threatening object. As it would go, Underdog was usually introduced with the following lines, "Look, in the sky! It's a plane! It's a bird! It's a frog! Not plane, nor bird, nor even frog. It's just little ol' me, Underdog" (Mouse FX, 2013)! Not sass, nor gun, nor even disrespect, it's just little ol' me, and I want to live. The lesson here is that what and who we see can either be cause for celebration, admiration, love, and respect, or something and someone to be feared and destroyed.

Scene 3: "Philosophical Questions"

In 1978, Black lesbian cultural worker and poet, Pat Parker, emphatically asked, "Where will you be when they come?" Through poetry, she ran through the genealogy of difference justifying death, of doctrine ruling the trigger/voting fingers of well-intentioned citizens. She theorized the evolution of hate, white supremacy, and heteropatriarchy in a series of statements beginning with, "It won't matter if…" Continuing Parker's line of questioning and critique via poetry, in 2007, Chinese-Jamaican slam poet activist Staceyann Chin in "All Oppression is Connected" urges:

the powers that have always been/have already come for the Jew
the communist/and the trade unionist/the time to act is now! Now!
while there are still ways we can fight/Now! because the rights we have
are still so very few
Now! because it is the right thing to do/Now! before you open the door
to find
they have finally come/for you

A common philosophical thought experiment goes, "If a tree falls in the forest and nobody is around to hear it, does it make a sound?" Following in this tradition, we – two Blackqueer poets, cultural workers, and scholar-artists – ask: If a Black person dies at the hands of a police officer and it's shot on camera, does justice get served? If a Black person is harmed in schools and an educator witnesses it, does equity ever happen? If a Black person says, "I can't breathe" and you hear them, does your application of force lessen? If a Black person is unarmed but you thought your life was in imminent danger and procedure permits lethal force, does a comb, phone, or Black hand morph into a gun? If Black activists, organizers, and youth advocate for gun reform but are dismissed as isolationists, disorganized, and misguided, and then a shooting happens in a predominately white suburb, does reform become a priority? If a Black person says that education is killing their spirit, what's the response of educators? If a bullet falls in a Black person, does it make a sound?

Returning to Pat Parker, we leave you here with the same sentiments. Where will you be, teacher, when they come? Where will you be, researcher, when they come? Where will you be? *Who Look at Me* (Jordan, 1969) still rings true today. Who looks? Who sees? We are Black, alive, and looking back at you.

REFLECTION QUESTIONS & INTERACTIVE EXERCISE

Now that you have had a chance to journey through this entire book, we want to return back to our initial reflection, charting the differences in our thinking now. Take note of these, and reflect on the following:

General Questions

- How would you describe your current gaze? What were your first thoughts when thinking about Blackness and queerness? What are they now?
- What are the ways you see Blackness and queerness in conversation with your working and everyday worlds? How has this changed after reading this text?

For Educators

- When thinking about those youth with whom you regularly engage, what qualities about their identities do you automatically notice? Which ones are you paying closer attention to now?

- How does Blackness and queerness show up in your educational space?
- In what ways are you considering showing up in your pedagogy differently?

Workshops

For deeper engagement, consider one of the workshops we facilitate in spaces interested in but not limited to: sustaining community, exploring identity, thinking through changing needs in groups, collective research methods, and art as activism. A sample of our workshop offerings follows. All workshops are 150–180 minutes in length and can be found at www.hilllwaters.com.

The Art and Power of "Weaving Our We"[19] is a three-part workshop series designed to introduce the methodological approach of collective auto/ethnography and to practice the art of story weaving. As part of the series, attendees are paired or grouped, and engage in a collaboration process from brainstorming to collective devising. These sequential workshops build upon each other; the first session emphasizes foundational principles and exercises of establishing roots for collective auto/ethnography, and the last focuses on devising.

Guiding questions: What relationship dynamics are essential to productively doing collective auto/ethnography? Why might a couple or group come to the practice of story weaving and/or collective auto/ethnography? How is collective auto/ethnography conducted?

Objectives

- Introduce participants to collaborative/collective writing practices
- Understand and define collective auto/ethnography
- Identify challenges to doing and writing collective auto/ethnography within ourselves
- Provide exercises and practices that help channel and transmute individual narratives into a collective telling

Erasing Boundaries, Building Bridges[20] is an interactive workshop which challenges stereotypes, questions privilege, and illuminates the "dirty work" involved in creating and sustaining community toward social justice.

Fundamental to this workshop is a rejection of political correctness, an approach which embraces tolerance. Instead, this workshop centers difference as strength and acknowledges it as a complex force that shapes our identities and interactions with the world, as well as a necessary ingredient for creating positive social change. Participants will gain tools and methodologies for erasing boundaries and building bridges across groups of difference, including acknowledging and navigating structural inequities, particularly as related to race, gender, sexuality, and class. This workshop is an experience-based venture using artistic tools that include but are not limited to poetry, movement, and theater exercises.

Guiding questions: What perceived differences shape intrapersonal and interpersonal engagement in community and group building? How do these differences connect and therefore serve as keys to sustaining community?

Objectives

- Name perceived boundaries between participants
- Identify tangible ways to continue eradicating boundaries within the group
- Construct a working vision of community with participants
- Introduce and facilitate exercises that foster vulnerability and deep connection
- Generate a new working agreement for working together

Building and Sustaining Critical Coalitions[21] is an experience-based interactive workshop geared toward groups seeking to address a particular concern or shift (e.g., LGBTQ group membership is increasingly including more trans-of-color individuals), and/or seeking to strengthen themselves around a particular issue or dynamic (e.g., intersectional inclusivity in racial affinity groups). Drawing upon Black feminist theory and queer-of-color theories, as well as artistic tools including poetry, movement, and theater exercises, this workshop helps groups become unstuck in a particular area of their work. By working through a recurring issue, concern of the group, or proactively strategizing around a foresight of the group, participants will leave with tools for addressing intergroup conflict in ways that account for power, voice, and identity.

Guiding questions: What are the requirements for coalition building? How might working through and acknowledging stereotyping, privilege, and cultural differences lead to strong and sustainable coalitions?

Objectives

- Identify key issue, concern, or initiative in need of addressing
- Name strengths and assets of the group (especially those that can assist our process)
- Construct a working vision of community with participants
- Devise a working plan for addressing initiative, concern, or issue

NOTES

[1] In reference to Harvey Young's (2010) articulation of the scene and seen of Blackness.

[2] In reference to *Black Panther* (2018), directed by Ryan Coogler and produced by Kevin Feige.

[3] In reference to *Black Panther* (2018), directed by Ryan Coogler and produced by Kevin Feige.

[4] *Underdog*, an animated series, debuted in 1964. See Biggers (1964).

[5] *Underdog*, an animated series, debuted in 1964. See Biggers (1964).

[6] See Paul Laurence Dunbar's (2003) poem, "We Wear the Mask."

[7] In reference to Stephon Clark (Levenson, Park, & Simon, 2018).

[8] In reference to Amadou Diallo (Cooper, 1999).

[9] In reference to Saheed Vassell (Rose, 2018).

[10] In reference to Tamir Rice (Shapiro, 2015).

[11] In reference to Sandra Bland (Sanchez, 2015).

[12] In reference to Victor White III (Rappleye, 2014).

[13] In reference to Freddie Gray (Karimi, Berryman, & Ford, 2016).

[14] In reference to Brennan Walker (Doubek, 2018) and Renisha McBride (Semuels, 2014).

[15] In reference to Walter Scott (Kinnard, 2017).

[16] In reference to Rekia Boyd (Schmadeke, St. Clair, & Gorner, 2013).

[17] In reference to Korryn Gaines (Lowery, 2016; Salinger, 2016) and Cliven Bundy (Keeler, 2014). It is important to note that we are not arguing for or against sovereignty and are not seeking to unfold the messy and complicated history of sovereignty claims within the United States. Instead, we merely highlight here the differences in how declarations of citizen sovereignty are taken up and respected, and in which the loss of life is not always the immediate outcome, even when armed.

[18] In reference to the ways that Black youth are generally seen as less innocent than their white peers, and are mistaken for, viewed, and treated as adults. Black children are not seen as children. See Epstein, Blake, and González (2017); Goff et al. (2014); Patton (2014); Shapiro (2017).

[19] This workshop can be run as a full series or offered as a single, condensed seminar.

[20] This workshop is especially beneficial for building & strengthening intercultural and leadership groups.

[21] This workshop is especially beneficial for building & strengthening intercultural and leadership groups.

EPILOGUE

Concerned with documenting the Freedom Struggles of the 1950's and 1960's, James Baldwin professed himself to be a witness (1968). His witnessing provided insights into both the site and sight (McKittrick, 2006) of Black cultural experiences and expression as lived within and in spite of the systematic ways Blackness was reduced to the abject and expendable. Notably, and as we close our meditation on considering how we see and do not see Blackness, Baldwin like Jordan was interested in how Black bodies were read, appraised, and consequently treated. Two of his works, "My Dungeon Shook: Letter to My Nephew on the One Hundredth Anniversary of the Emancipation" and "A Talk to Teachers," both originally published as magazine periodicals, take up sociological and educational gazes as they affix to Black bodies and Black youth in particular. As contemporaries, Baldwin and Jordan take seriously structural imposition in/on Black lives and even more so Black folks' creativity in the face of these barriers. More specifically they recognize the genius and intellectual capacities of youth to understand and critique texts—literary and artistic—that represent and illustrate the complex nature of their social worlds. Following this belief, *The Fire Next Time* (1962), a collection of reflective biographical narratives and essays, provides a letter written to Baldwin's (fictitious) nephew. In his letter, Baldwin outlines the sociological gaze mapped upon his nephew's Black body, and provides a rather queer familial relationship – the queering of Black masculinity, and Black men/boy relationships to and longing for one another. The queerness of the text is seen through an understanding of how Black people have been surrendered to the peripheries of society:

> This innocent country set you down in a ghetto in which, in fact, it intended that you should perish. Let me spell out precisely what I mean by that, for the heart of the matter is here, and the root of my dispute with my country. You were born where you were born and faced the future that you faced because you were black and for no other reason. The limits of your ambition were, thus, expected to be set forever. You were born into a society which spelled out with brutal clarity, and in as many ways as possible, that you were a worthless human being. (Baldwin, 1998, p. 293)

© KONINKLIJKE BRILL NV, LEIDEN, 2019 | DOI:10.1163/9789004392243_008

The text also provides another queer reading: the demonstration of a "feeling of, feeling for" one another between Black men and boys (Tinsley, 2008, p. 192). We are welcomed into an impossibility and oft rare vulnerability of love between Black boys/men. Nowhere is this more apparent than in Baldwin's (1998) continued focus on love and loving his nephew, in which he says, "here you were: to be loved. To be loved, baby, hard, at once, and forever, to strengthen you against the loveless world" (p. 293). He continues with a reminder of the possibility of love, of a loving gaze to circumvent the societal gaze. "Remember that: I know how black it looks today, for you. It looked bad that day, too, yes, we were trembling. We have not stopped trembling yet, but if we had not loved each other none of us would have survived" (p. 293). Holding fast to love, Baldwin (1962) leaves us with a promise. "And now you must survive because we love you, and for the sake of your children and your children's children" (p. 293). It is with this promise in mind, and with the reality of how "black it [still] looks today," that we close this book.

In our contemporary black state of affairs, Baldwin's prescient words to teachers still ring true, that "any citizen of this country who figures himself as responsible – and particularly those of you who deal with the minds and hearts of young people – must be prepared to 'go for broke'" (Baldwin, 1998, p. 678). Published within a year of one another, we see both the educational and sociological gazes which Black youth endure illustrated through Baldwin's works. His critical analysis not only offers us ways to understand the sinister crisis of identity, myth, and hate,[1] but also ways to work against the appraisal of Black bodies, and of his Black nephew in particular, as less than, as only being able to aspire to mediocrity, as a myth and scorn of hate. In the throes of a contemporary moment of needed revolution and change, the poignant immediacy of Baldwin's wisdom for a present past felt necessary for us. What follows is a staged conversation between a fictive queer past and present. Continuing with the epistolary tradition used throughout this book, we close with a letter to our beloved Uncle Jimmy, an affectionate name given as honor to James Baldwin and shared across afro-diasporic communities, a recognition of queer kin. We offer this letter as a means of talking with Baldwin, letting the world, inclusive of and specifically towards teachers, listen in on our conversation. Moreover, and indicative of a final thought for June Jordan's questions, "who look" and "who see" (Jordan, 1969, p. 7), we answer here: love looks, love sees.

DEAR UNCLE JIMMY

Thank you for your letter. In the three-year span between finishing undergraduate school and co-teaching my first undergraduate course, Introduction to Black World Studies, I read and reread your words at least four times. I cannot remember how I first received it, but I recall sitting with it, imagining the fire rising as you divulged a lesson that you felt the youth coming after you, your family, should know. Each time I found something new, all the while wondering what you might explicitly say to me, your niece. I didn't receive your letter until much later, sometime during my graduate studies, I took a course devoted to the breadth of your works. The class was full of our countrymen who were still innocent and still in need of seeing themselves and me differently. I remember feeling so profoundly aware that some of the meaning of your words escaped them, the passage of time and perhaps more importantly having a frame of context in which you wrote alluded them. Like a love note passed about a classroom for which I had the decoder, you were speaking directly to me. And since it is rude to not speak when spoken to, we write to you on the sunset of this country's celebration of Independence Day, still 100 years too soon.

More than 50 years have passed since you wrote to us, your kin, and talked to teachers. Our society still refuses to "go for broke" as you urged.[2] We are, however, going broke, but not because we have shown ourselves willing to be responsible citizens. Eight-year-old children are committing suicide, with one child we know of choosing school as his site of surrender.[3] A teacher receives a minimal monetary fine for her decision to cut Lamya's braided and beaded hair, and she is not the only Black child whose body is marked a problematic site/sight.[4] Kelley Williams-Bolar, a single Black mother with housing insecurity, was jailed for daring to put her kids in a better school, a school with more resources, a predominantly white school.[5] So much for Brown v. Board and access to quality education, huh Uncle Jimmy?

Back when you wrote "A Talk to Teachers," the 1954 desegregation case was a toddler. We know there were plenty of Black schools and Black women teachers – many of whom lost their jobs with desegregation – but who did you imagine these teachers to be? We surmised the room you placed yourself in was packed wall-to-wall with countrymen's wives and daughters. You wanted them to know the stakes of Black youth growing up in the conditions to which they are subjected, as well as the undetectable (to the untrained and uninterested eye) weight carried. We also imagine that you hoped these teachers would take responsibility for history and recognize education in classrooms as one space to undermine and work against the legacies that helped build this country. By exposing all children to truth and therefore possibility, we, like you, could remain hopeful.

Over time, however, we frequently find our aspirations seized. You said, "One of the paradoxes of education was that precisely at the point when you begin to develop a conscience, you must find yourself at war with your society" (p. 679), and we have found ourselves deep in those trenches. At times, it has felt that our particular conscience is one which has not been shared broadly enough by our countrymen. We wonder if the scarcity of an education that incites awareness is cause (or source) for the symptoms named earlier. Perhaps therein lies the problem: underdeveloped consciences. Is this why the war against society wanes? We must conclude that if education that generated an awakening (in mind and body, theory and action) to the world around us, to the hypocrisy of our country, and to the greater danger of pretending not to see, was less a rarity, the idea of being unfree would implore refusal, collective human resistance, and the will to "make America what America must become" (Baldwin, 1998, p. 294).

We contend that for America to become something new requires vision and an ability to see it, its people, and its history differently. This, Uncle Jimmy is the productive potential of gaze. Over the last couple of years, we have waded through various lenses used to see and mis-see Black bodies. Even more fervently, though, we have demanded that our bodies, through performance, and writing are seen on our terms. We are placing our experiences of gaze as an oppressive technology in conversation with freedom rehearsals. Because of you and many of your friends (and would-be friends) like Lorraine, Zora, Pat, Audre, June, Bayard, bell, and Nikky, there are examples for us to follow and retool. From embarking upon a journey together of minding and mending the fallout of gaze and its misuse, our sensibilities about the crisis of identity of which you repeatedly speak are deepening and our understanding about the work to come is clearer.

As your kin, as the children you pleaded for your country to see as human, and now as educators who choose routinely to see Blackness, queerness, and the people who embody them in their full scope, we know viscerally the residual effects of terrible educations, the eerie, itchy feeling induced from being the target of gawking. We also know that these moments provide sight. Because of you and many like you, some of whom we have named and some of whose names we know not, we sense that there is another way forward, another way to be seen. That way is love. We are not certain if you knew how much your words would mean one day to some far-distant niece, nephew, kinfolk of yours, just as Black and queer as the moon hangs in the firmament. You found us, and because you and our ancestors loved us, we have survived. Thank you. For the generations to come, we echo here as Uncle Jimmy and Sweet Lorraine have, because we have known love, because we love you, you too will survive, as will your children's children's children. Perhaps this is all we can ever offer the future: a vision of love, loving gazes, seeing our survival as predicated upon our capacity to be loving, and loving our children into a future that doesn't demand the death of someone else's child so they might live. Love. Love. Love.

With all our love,

Hill L. Waters

NOTES

[1] Within the essay, Baldwin notes that the sinister matter of the fact is that, "They really hate you – really hate you because in their eyes (and they're right) you stand between them and life. [...] It is the most sinister of the facts, I think, which we now face" (p. 681). Continuing to unpack this sinister fact, he also draws our attention to two myths, one about the identity of the republic, and the other about the identity of its citizens, in particular its white citizenry. Baldwin states, "[...] a price is demanded to liberate all those white children – some of them near forty – who have never grown up, and who never will grow up, because they have no sense of their identity. What passes for identity in America is a series of myths about one's heroic ancestors" (p. 683). These myths and the most sinister of facts also belies another crisis: "I had been invented by white people, and I knew enough about life by this time to understand that whatever you invent, whatever you project, is you! So where we are now is that a whole country of people believe I'm a 'nigger,' and I don't, and the battle's on! Because if I am not what I've been told I am, then it means that you're not what you thought you were either! And that is the crisis" (p. 682).

[2] See Baldwin (1998).

[3] See http://www.orlandosentinel.com/features/education/os-gun-suicide-school-campus-seminole-20150225-story.html

[4] See blackgirllonghair.com/2009/12/milwaukee-teacher-cuts-off-little-girls-natural-hair-as-punishment-throws-it-away-in-front-of-her/

[5] See https://www.nytimes.com/2011/09/27/us/jailed-for-switching-her-daughters-school-district.html

REFERENCES

Alexander, B. K. (2000). Skin flint (or, the garbage man's kid): A generative autobiographical performance based on Tami Spry's tattoo stories. *Text and Performance Quarterly, 20*(1), 97–114.

Alexander, B. K. (2006a). Performance and pedagogy. In D. S. Madison & J. Hamera (Eds.), *The Sage handbook of performance studies* (pp. 253–260). Thousand Oaks, CA: Sage Publications.

Alexander, B. K. (2006b). *Performing Black masculinity: Race, culture, and queer identity.* Lanham, MD: AltaMira Press.

Alexander, B. K. (2011). Standing in the wake: A critical auto/ethnographic exercise on reflexivity in three movements. *Cultural Studies ⇔ Critical Methodologies, 11*(2), 98–107.

Alexander, B. K., Moreira, C., & Kumar, H. S. (2012). Resisting (resistance) stories: A tri-autoethnographic exploration of father narratives across shades of difference. *Qualitative Inquiry, 18*(2), 121–133.

Alexander, E. (1994). "Can you be Black and look at this?" Reading the Rodney King video(s). *Public Culture, 7*(1), 77–94.

Alexander, M. J. (2005). *Pedagogies of crossing: Meditations on feminism, sexual politics, memory, and the sacred.* Durham, NC: Duke University Press.

Anderson, L. (2006). Analytic autoethnography. *Journal of Contemporary Ethnography, 35*(4), 373–395.

Anderson, L. M. (2008). *Black feminism in contemporary drama.* Urbana, IL: University of Illinois Press.

Angrosino, M. (2008). Recontextualizing observation: Ethnography, pedagogy, and the prospects for a progressive political agenda. In N. Denzin & Y. Lincoln (Eds.), *Collecting and interpreting qualitative materials* (pp. 161–184). Thousand Oaks, CA: Sage Publications.

Aronson, B. A., & Boveda, M. (2017). The intersection of White supremacy and the education industrial complex: An analysis of #BlackLivesMatter and the criminalization of people with disabilities. *Journal of Educational Controversy, 12*(1), 6.

Baldwin, J. (1962). *The fire next time.* New York, NY: Vintage Books.

Baldwin, J. (1968). *The amen corner.* New York, NY: The Dial Press.

Baldwin, J. (1985). *The evidence of things not seen.* New York, NY: Holt, Rinehart, and Winston.

Baldwin, J. (1998). A talk to teachers. In T. Morrison (Ed.), *Baldwin: Collected essay* (pp. 678–686). New York, NY: Library of America. (Reprinted from *Saturday Review*, 1963)

Baldwin, J. (1998). My dungeon shook: Letter to my nephew. In T. Morrison (Ed.), *Baldwin: Collected essay* (pp. 291–295). New York, NY: Library of America. (Reprinted from *The Progressive*, 1962)

Bambara, T. C. (1969). On the issue of roles. In T. C. Bambara (Ed.), *The Black woman: An anthology* (pp. 123–135). New York, NY: Washington Square Press.

Bambara, T. C. (1980). *The salt eaters.* New York, NY: Random House.

Bambara, T. C. (1996). The education of a storyteller. In T. Morrison (Ed.), *Deep sightings and rescue missions: Fiction, essays, and conversations* (pp. 246–255). New York, NY: Pantheon Books.

Bambara, T. C. (2009). *Deep sightings & rescue missions: Fiction, essays, and conversations.* New York, NY: Vintage Books.

Beam, J. (1986). *In the life: A Black gay anthology.* Boston, MA: Alyson Publications.

Behar, R. (1996). *The vulnerable observer: Anthropology that breaks your heart.* Boston, MA: Beacon Press.

Bell, E. (1995). Toward a pleasure-centered economy: Wondering a feminist aesthetics of performance. *Text and Performance Quarterly, 15*(2), 99–121.

Beyoncé. (2013, December 13). *Drunk in love* [Recorded by Beyoncé ft. Jay-Z]. New York, NY: Parkwood Entertainment/Columbia.

Biggers, W. W. (Producer). (1964). *Underdog* [Television series]. New York, NY: National Broadcasting Company.

Blackburn, M. V. (2007). The experiencing, negotiation, breaking, and remaking of gender rules and regulations by queer youth. *Journal of Gay & Lesbian Issues in Education, 4*(2), 33–54.

Black Girl with Long Hair. (2009, December 14). *Milwaukee teacher cuts off little girl's natural hair as punishment, throws it away in front of her.* Retrieved from http://blackgirllonghair.com/2009/12/milwaukee-teacher-cuts-off-little-girls-natural-hair-as-punishment-throws-it-away-in-front-of-her/

Boal, A. (1985). *Theatre of the oppressed.* New York, NY: Theatre Communications Group.

Bochner, A., & Ellis, C. (2016). *Evocative autoethnography: Writing lives and telling stories.* New York, NY: Routledge.

Bolen, D. M. (2012). *Toward an applied communication relational inquiry: Autoethnography, co-constructed narrative, and relational futures* (Unpublished doctoral dissertation). Wayne State University, Detroit, MI.

Boylorn, R. M. (2006). E pluribus unum (out of many, one). *Qualitative Inquiry, 12*(4), 651–680.

Boylorn, R. M. (2008). As seen on TV: An autoethnographic reflection on race and reality television. *Critical Studies in Media Communication, 25*(4), 413–433.

Boylorn, R. M. (2011). Gray or for colored girls who are tired of chasing rainbows: Race and reflexivity. *Cultural Studies ⇔ Critical Methodologies, 11*(2), 178–186.

Boylorn, R. M. (2012). Dark-skinned love stories. *International Review of Qualitative Research, 5*(3), 299–309.

Boylorn, R. M. (2013a). "Sit with your legs closed!" and other sayin's from my childhood. In. S. Holman Jones, T. E. Adams, & C. Ellis (Eds.), *Handbook of autoethnography* (pp. 173–185). Walnut Creek, CA: Left Coast Press.

Boylorn, R. M. (2013b). *Sweetwater: Black women and narratives of resilience.* New York, NY: Peter Lang.

Boylorn, R. M., & Orbe, M. P. (Eds.). (2014). *Critical autoethnography: Intersecting cultural identities in everyday life.* Walnut Creek, CA: Left Coast Press.

Brockenbrough, E. (2013). Introduction to the special issue: Queers of color and anti-oppressive knowledge production. *Curriculum Inquiry, 43*(4), 426–440.

Brockenbrough, E. (2015). Queer of color agency in educational contexts: Analytic frameworks from a queer of color critique. *Educational Studies, 51*(1), 28–44.

Brown, A. B., & Clift, J. W. (2010). The unequal effect of adequate yearly progress: Evidence from school visits. *American Education Research Journal, 47*(4), 774–798.

Brown, R. N. (2009). *Black girlhood celebration: Toward a hip-hop feminist pedagogy.* New York, NY: Peter Lang.

Brown, R. N. (2013). *Hear our truths: The creative potential of Black girlhood.* Urbana, IL: University of Illinois Press.

Brown, R. N. (2013, October 16). *Hear our truths: The creative potential of Black girlhood, by Ruth Nicole Brown* [Video File]. Urbana, IL: University of Illinois Press. Retrieved from https://www.youtube.com/watch?v=OomZIYFmFkE

Brown, R. N. (2014). She came at me wreckless! Wreckless theatrics as disruptive methodology. In R. N. Brown, R. Carducci, & C. R. Kuby (Eds.), *Disruptive qualitative inquiry: Possibilities and tensions in educational research* (pp. 35–52). New York, NY: Peter Lang.

Brown, R. N., Carducci, R., & Kuby, C. R. (Eds.). (2014). *Disrupting qualitative inquiry: Possibilities and tensions in educational research.* New York, NY: Peter Lang.

Brown, R. N., & Kwakye, C. J. (Eds.). (2012). *Wish to live: The hip-hop feminism pedagogy reader.* New York, NY: Peter Lang.

Byrd, R. P., Cole, J. B., & Guy-Sheftall, B. (Eds.). (2009). *I am your sister: Collected and unpublished writings of Audre Lorde.* Oxford: Oxford University Press.

Cacho, L. M. (2007). "You just don't know how much he meant:" Deviancy, death and devaluation. *Latino Studies, 5*(2), 182–208.

Cacho, L. M. (2011). Racialized hauntings of the devalued dead. In G. K. Hong & R. A. Ferguson (Eds.), *Strange affinities: The gender and sexual politics of comparative racialization* (pp. 25–52). Durham, NC: Duke University Press.

Callier, D. M. (2008). *Dirty work* [poem]. (Unpublished manuscript)

Callier, D. M. (2011). A call to love: In remembrance of our quare saints. *Qualitative Research Journal, 11*(2), 85–94.

Callier, D. M. (2012). Acting OUT: A performative exploration of identity, healing, and wholeness. In R. N. Brown & C. J. Kwakye (Eds.), *Wish to live: The hip-hop feminism pedagogy reader* (pp. 141–161). New York, NY: Peter Lang.

Callier, D. M. (2013). Tell it: A contemporary chorale for Black youth voices. In M. E. Weems (Ed.), *Writings of healing and resistance: Empathy and the imagination intellect.* New York, NY: Peter Lang.

Callier, D. M. (2016). Sakia Gunn, Joseph Walker Hoover, and Gendered Violences: Queer of color critiques in educational spaces. In H. Greenhalgh-Spencer (Ed.), *Gender and education section of M. Peters (Ed.),: The encyclopedia of educational philosophy and theory.* Dordrecht: Springer. doi:10.1007/978-981-287-532-7_429-1

Callier, D. M. (2016). *Staging [in]visible subjects: Blackqueer bodies, social death and performance* (Doctoral dissertation). University of Illinois Press, Urbana, IL.

Callier, D. M. (2018). Still, nobody mean more: Engaging Black feminist pedagogies on questions of the citizen and human in anti-Blackqueer times. *Curriculum Inquiry, 48*(1), 16–34.

Callier, D. M., Hill, D. C., & Waters, H. L. (2017a). Answering the call. *International Review of Qualitative Research, 10*(1), 13–21.

Callier, D. M., Hill, D. C., & Waters, H. L. (2017b). Critical collaborative performance autoethnography. In S. L. Pensoneau-Conway, T. E. Adams, & D. M. Bolen (Eds.), *Doing autoethnography* (pp. 37–44). Rotterdam, The Netherlands: Sense Publishers.

Campbell, S. L. (2012). For colored girls? Factors that influence teacher recommendations into advanced courses for Black girls. *The Review of Black Political Economy, 39*(4), 389–402.

Carlson, M. (1996). *Performance: A critical introduction.* New York, NY: Routledge.

Carroll, R. (1997). *Sugar in the raw: Voices of young Black girls in America*. New York, NY: Random House.

Carter, P. L. (2005). *Keepin' it real: School success beyond Black and White*. New York, NY: Oxford University Press.

Castagno, P. C. (2001). *New playwriting strategies: A language-based approach to playwriting*. New York, NY: Routledge.

Chang, H. (2008). *Autoethnography as method*. Walnut Creek, CA: Left Coast Press.

Chang, H., & Boyd, D. (Eds.). (2011). *Spirituality in higher education: Autoethnographies*. Thousand Oaks, CA: Left Coast Press.

Chin, S. [Culture Project]. (2007, November 18). *Opening celebration (Part 16): Staceyann Chin* [Video File]. Retrieved from

Cobb, J. (2013, July 13). George Zimmerman, not guilty: Blood on the leaves. *The New Yorker*. Retrieved from http://www.newyorker.com/news/news-desk/george-zimmerman-not-guilty-blood-on-the-leaves

Cobb, J. (2014, November 25). Chronicle of a riot foretold. *The New Yorker*. Retrieved from http://www.newyorker.com/news/daily-comment/chronicle-ferguson-riot-michael-brown

Cohen, C. J. (1997). Punks, bulldaggers, and welfare queens: The radical potential of queer politics? *GLQ: A Journal of Lesbian and Gay Studies, 3*(4), 437–465.

Cohen, C. J. (1999). What is this movement doing to my politics? *Social Text, 17*(4), 111–118.

Cohen, C. J. (2004). Deviance as resistance: A new research agenda for the study of Black politics. *Du Bois Review: Social Science Research on Race, 1*(1), 27–45.

Cohen, C. J. (2010). Death and rebirth of a movement: Queering critical ethnic studies. *Social Justice, 37*(4), 126–132.

Collins, P. H. (1990). *Black feminist thought: Knowledge consciousness and the politics of empowerment*. New York, NY: Routledge.

Combahee River Collective. (1979). Six Black women: Why did they die. *Radical America, 13*(6), 44–46.

Conquergood, D. (1991). Rethinking ethnography: Towards a critical cultural politics. *Communication Monographs, 58*(2), 179–194.

Conquergood, D. (2002). Performance studies: Interventions and radical research. *The Drama Review, 46*(2), 145–156.

Conquergood, D. (2006). Rethinking ethnography: Towards a critical cultural politics. In D. S. Madison & J. Hamera (Eds.), *The Sage handbook of performance studies* (pp. 351–365). Thousand Oaks, CA: Sage Publications.

Cooper, M. (1999, February 5). Officers in Bronx fire 41 shots, and an unarmed man is killed. *The New York Times*. Retrieved from https://www.nytimes.com/1999/02/05/nyregion/officers-in-bronx-fire-41-shots-and-an-unarmed-man-is-killed.html

Cox, A. M. (2015). *Shapeshifters: Black girls and the choreography of citizenship*. Durham, NC: Duke University Press.

Crenshaw, K. (1991). Mapping the margins: Intersectionality, identity politics, and violence against women of color. *Stanford Law Review, 43*(6), 1241–1299.

Crenshaw, K., Ocen, P., & Nanda, J. (2015). *Black girls matter: Pushed out, overpoliced, and underprotected*. New York, NY: Center for Intersectionality and Social Policy Studies. Retrieved from https://static1.squarespace.com/static/53f20d90e4b0b80451158d8c/t/54d2d37ce4b024b41443b0ba/1423102844010/BlackGirlsMatter_Report.pdf

Davies, B., & Bansel, P. (2007). Neoliberalism and education. *International Journal of Qualitative Studies in Education, 20*(3), 247–259.

Deck, A. A. (1990). Autoethnography: Zora Neale Hurston, Noni Jabavu, and cross-disciplinary discourse. *Black American Literature Forum, 24*(2), 237–256.

DeFrantz, T. F., & Gonzalez, A. (Eds.). (2014). *Black performance theory*. Durham, NC: Duke University Press.

Delamont, S. (2007, September 5–8). *Arguments against auto-ethnography*. Paper presented at the British Educational Research Association Annual Conference, Institute of Education, University of London, London.

Deming, B. (1974). *We cannot live without our lives*. New York, NY: Grossman Publishers.

Denzin, N. K. (1989). *Interpretive biography*. Newbury Park, CA: Sage Publications.

Denzin, N. K. (1997). *Interpretive ethnography: Ethnographic practices for the 21st century*. Thousand Oaks, CA: Sage Publications.

Denzin, N. K. (2003). *Performance ethnography: Critical pedagogy and the politics of culture*. Thousand Oaks, CA: Sage Publications.

Denzin, N. K., & Lincoln, Y. S. (2002). *The qualitative inquiry reader*. Thousand Oaks, CA: Sage Publications.

Denzin, N. K., & Lincoln, Y. S. (Eds.). (2008). *Collecting and interpreting qualitative materials*. Thousand Oaks, CA: Sage Publications.

Denzin, N. K., Lincoln, Y. S., & Smith, L. T. (2008). *Handbook of critical indigenous methodologies*. Thousand Oaks, CA: Sage Publications.

Diamond, E. (1996). Introduction. In E. Diamond (Ed.), *Performance and cultural politics* (pp. 1–12). New York, NY: Routledge

Dickar, M. (2008). *Corridor cultures: Mapping student resistance at an urban high school*. New York, NY: New York University Press.

Dillard, C. B. (2012). *Learning to (re)member the things we've learned to forget: Endarkened feminisms, spirituality, and the sacred nature of research and teaching*. New York, NY: Peter Lang.

Dillard, C. B. (2016). We are still here: Declarations of love and sovereignty in Black life under siege. *Educational Studies, 52*(3), 201–215.

Dillard, C. B., & Okpalaoka, C. (2011). The sacred and spiritual nature of endarkened transnational feminist praxis in qualitative research. In N. K. Denzin & Y. S. Lincoln (Eds.), *The Sage handbook of qualitative research* (pp. 147–162). Thousand Oaks, CA: Sage Publications.

Diversi, M., & Moreira, C. (2009). *Betweener talk: Decolonizing knowledge production, pedagogy, and praxis*. Walnut Creek, CA: Left Coast Press.

Doubek, A. (2018, April 15). Black teenager shot at after asking for directions. *National Public Radio*. Retrieved from https://www.npr.org/sections/thetwo-way/2018/04/15/602598119/black-teenager-shot-at-after-asking-for-directions

Dunbar, P. L. (1993). *The collected poetry of Paul Laurence Dunbar*. Charlottesville, VA: University of Virginia Press.

Durham, A. (2003). Holloween, the morning-after poem. *Qualitative Inquiry, 9*(2), 300–302. doi:10.1177/1077800403009002012

Durham, A. (2004). Verbal exchange. *Qualitative Inquiry, 10*(4), 493–494. doi:10.1177/1077800403259699

Durham, A. (2014). *Home with hip hop feminism*. New York, NY: Peter Lang.

Durham, A. (2017). On collards. *International Review of Qualitative Research, 10*(1), 22–23.

Eisner, E. W. (2003). Questionable assumptions about schooling. *Phi Delta Kappan, 84*(9), 648–657.

Eisner, E. W. (2006). Does arts-based research have a future? *Studies in Art Education, 48*(1), 9–18.

Eisner, E. W. (2009). What education can learn from the arts. *Art Education, 62*(1), 6–9.

Ellingson, L. L. (2017). *Embodiment in qualitative research.* New York, NY: Routledge.

Ellis, C., & Bochner, A. P. (Eds.). (1996). Taking ethnography into the twenty-first century [Special issue]. *Journal of Contemporary Ethnography, 25*(1), 3–5.

Emdin, C. (2011). Moving beyond the boat without a paddle: Reality pedagogy, Black youth, and urban science education. *The Journal of Negro Education, 80*, 284–295.

Emdin, C. (2012). Reality pedagogy and urban science education: Towards a comprehensive understanding of the urban science classroom. In B. J. Fraser, K. G. Tobin, & C. J. McRobbie (Eds.), *Second international handbook of science education* (pp. 59–68). Dordrecht: Springer.

Epstein, R., Blake, J., & González, T. (2017). *Girlhood interrupted: The erasure of Black girls' childhood.* Retrieved from https://dx.doi.org/10.2139/ssrn.3000695

Evans-Winters, V. (2005). *Teaching Black girls: Resiliency in urban classrooms.* New York, NY: Peter Lang.

Fanon, F., Sartre, J. P., & Farrington, C. (1963). *The wretched of the earth* (Vol. 36). New York, NY: Grove Press.

Feige, K. (Producer), & Coogler, R. (Director). (2018). *Black panther* [Motion picture]. Glendale, CA: Marvel Pictures.

Fleetwood, N. R. (2011). *Troubling vision: Performance, visuality, and blackness.* Chicago, IL: University of Chicago Press.

Fogg-Davis, H. G. (2006). Theorizing Black lesbians within Black feminism: A critique of same-race street harassment. *Politics & Gender, 2*(1), 57–76.

Fordham, S. (1993). "Those loud Black girls": (Black) women, silence, and gender "passing" in the academy. *Anthropology and Education Quarterly, 24*(1), 3–32.

Fordham, S., & Ogbu, J. U. (1986). Black students' school success: Coping with the "burden of 'acting White.'" *The Urban Review, 18*(3), 176–206.

Forrest, S. (2009, February 9). Book corner: Celebrating Black girlhood in a contradictory culkture explored. *Illinois News Bureau.* Retrieved from https://news.illinois.edu/view/6367/210514

Franklin, A. (2011, March 7). *Spirit in the dark* [Video File]. Retrieved from https://youtu.be/qvGmbsLxF0w

Freire, P. (1970). *Pedagogy of the oppressed.* New York, NY: The Continuum Publishing Company.

Freire, P. (1973). *Education for critical consciousness.* New York, NY: The Seabury Press.

French, A. (2012, March). Who I be when you look at me: SOLHOT part 1 [PDF document]. Retrieved from http://ashafrench.com/who-i-be-when-you-look-at-me-solhot-part-1/

Gale, K., Pelias, R., Russell, L., Spry, T., & Wyatt, J. (2013). Intensity. *International Review of Qualitative Research, 6*(1), 165–180.

Garner, P. (2011, February 2). Saving yourself first. *The Public I.* Retrieved from http://publici.ucimc.org/wp-content/uploads/2011/02/feb11.pdf

Garner, P. (2012). Check-in. In R. N. Brown & C. J. Kwakye (Eds.), *Wish to live: The hip-hop feminism pedagogy reader* (pp. 229–240). New York, NY: Peter Lang.

Gaunt, K. D. (2006). *The games Black girls play: Learning the ropes from double-dutch to hip-hop.* New York, NY: New York University Press.

Goff, P. A., Jackson, M. C., Leone, D., Lewis, B. A., Culotta, C. M., & DiTomasso, N. A. (2014). The essence of innocence: Consequences of dehumanizing Black children. *Journal of Personality and Social Psychology, 106*(4), 526.

Goodall, H. L. (2000). *Writing the new ethnography*. Walnut Creek, CA: AltaMira Press.

Goodman, A., & González, J. (2003, July 14). "It's a shame that you have to walk down the street not knowing what's going to happen to us": The Sakia Gunn murder. *Democracy Now!* Retrieved from http://www.democracynow.org/2003/7/14/its_a_shame_that_you_have

Gordon, A. P. (2005). Something more than skepticism. In L. J. Holmes & C. A. Wall (Eds.), *Savoring the salt: The legacy of Toni Cade Bambara* (pp. 256–272). Philadelphia, PA: Temple University Press.

Grant, L. (1994). Helpers, enforcers, and go-betweens: Black females in elementary school classrooms. In M. B. Zinn & B. T. Dill (Eds.), *Women of color in U.S. society*. Philadelphia, PA: Temple University Press.

Greene, M. (1995). *Releasing the imagination: Essays on education, the arts, and social change*. San Francisco, CA: Jossey-Bass.

Gumbs, A. P. (2010). We can learn to mother ourselves: The queer survival of Black feminism 1968–1996: Dissertation abstracts international, section A. *The Humanities and Social Sciences, 71*(4), 1299.

Gumbs, A. P. (2011). The zen of young money: Being present to the genius of Black youth. *Crunk Feminist Collective*. Retrieved from http://crunkfeministcollective.wordpress.com/2011/01/24/the-zen-of-young-money-being-present-to-the-genius-of-black-youth/

Gumbs, A. P. (2012). The shape of my impact. The Feminist Wire. Retrieved from http://www.thefeministwire.com/2012/10/the-shape-of-my-impact/

Gumbs, A. P. (2016). *Spill: Scenes of Black feminist fugitivity*. Durham, NC: Duke University Press.

Gutiérrez y Muhs, G., Niemann, Y. F., González, C. G., & Harris, A. P. (Eds.). (2012). *Presumed incompetent: The intersections of race and class for women in academia*. Boulder, CO: University Press of Colorado.

Halberstam, J. (2005). *In a queer time and place: Transgender bodies, subcultural lives*. New York, NY: New York University Press.

Halberstam, J. (2011). *The queer art of failure*. Durham, NC: Duke University Press.

Hamera, J., & Counqergood, D. (2006). Performance and politics: Themes and arguments. In D. S. Madison & J. Hamera (Eds.), *The Sage handbook of performance studies* (pp. 419–426). Thousand Oaks, CA: Sage Publications.

Hanhardt, C. B. (2013). *Safe space: Gay neighborhood history and the politics of violence*. Durham, NC: Duke University Press.

Hansberry, L. (1958). *A raisin in the sun*. New York, NY: Signet.

Hansberry, L. (1981). The Negro writer and his roots: Toward a new romanticism. *The Black Scholar, 12*(2), 2–12.

Hardt, M., & Negri, A. (2005). *Multitude: War and democracy in the age of empire*. New York, NY: Penguin.

Harris, E. L. (2005). *Freedom in this village: Twenty-five years of Black gay men's writing 1979 to the present*. New York, NY: Avalon Publishing Group.

Hartman, S. (2007). *Lose your mother: A journey along the Atlantic slave route*. New York, NY: Farrar, Straus, and Giroux.

Henry, A. (1998). 'Invisible' and 'womanish': Blackgirls negotiating their lives in an African-centered school in the USA. *Race Ethnicity and Education, 1*(2), 151–170.

Hill, D. C. (2008). Writing to right a wrong: Advocacy in qualitative inquiry. *Democracy and Education, 17*(3), 26–31.

Hill, D. C. (2013). *When it gets in the blood* [poem]. (Unpublished manuscript)

Hill, D. C. (2014a). *Transgressngroove: An exploration of Black girlhood, the body, and education.* Retrieved from http://search.proquest.com/docview/1652004256?accountid=14553

Hill, D. C. (2014b). A vulnerable disclosure: Dangerous negotiations of race and identity in the classroom. *Journal of Pedagogy, 5*(2), 161–181.

Hill, D. C. (2017). What happened when I invited students to see me? A Black queer professor's reflections on practicing embodied vulnerability in the classroom. *Journal of lesbian studies, 21*(4), 432–442.

Hill, D. C. (2018). Black girl pedagogies: layered lessons on reliability. *Curriculum Inquiry, 48*(3), 383–405. doi:10.1080/03626784.2018.1468213

Holland, S. P. (2000). *Raising the dead: Readings of death and (Black) subjectivity.* Durham, NC: Duke University Press.

Holman Jones, S. (2008). Performance and pedagogy. In N. K. Denzin & Y. S. Lincoln (Eds.), *Collecting and interpreting qualitative materials* (pp. 205–246). Thousand Oaks, CA: Sage Publications.

Holman Jones, S., Adams, T. E., & Ellis, C. (Eds.). (2013). *Handbook of autoethnography.* Walnut Creek, CA: Left Coast Press.

Holmes, K. A. (2011). *Chocolate to Rainbow City: The dialectics of Black and gay community formation in postwar Washington, DC, 1946–1978* (Doctoral dissertation). University of Illinois Press, Urbana, IL.

Holt, N. L. (2003). Representation, legitimation, and autoethnography: An autoethnographic writing story. *International Journal of Qualitative Methods, 2*(1), 1–24.

HomeGirlsHandMadeGrenades. (2015, October). *Just don't never give up on love* [Audio file]. Retrieved from https://soundcloud.com/hghmg/just-dont-never-give-up-on-love-mix-1

Hong, G. K., & Ferguson, R. A. (2011). Introduction. In G. K. Hong & R. A. Ferguson (Eds.), *Strange affinities: The gender and sexual politics of comparative racialization* (pp. 1–22). Durham, NC: Duke University Press.

hooks, b. (1990). *Yearning: Race, gender, and cultural politics.* Boston, MA: South End Press.

hooks, b. (1994). *Teaching to transgress: Education as the practice of freedom.* New York, NY: Routledge.

hooks, b. (1995a). *Art on my mind: Visual politics.* New York, NY: The New Press.

hooks, b. (1995b). Performance practice as a site of opposition. In C. Ugwu (Ed.), *Let's get it on: The politics of Black performance* (pp. 210–221). Seattle, WA: Bay Press.

hooks, b. (1996). *Bone Black: Memories of girlhood.* New York, NY: Henry Holt and Company.

hooks, b. (2000). *Feminist theory: From margin to center.* Cambridge, MA: South End Press.

hooks, b. (2001). *All about love: New visions.* New York, NY: Perennial.

hooks, b. (2003). *Teaching community: A pedagogy of hope.* New York, NY: Routledge.

hooks, b. (2004). *We real cool: Black men and masculinity.* New York, NY: Routledge.

Horvat, E. M., & Antonio, A. L. (1999). "Hey, those shoes are out of uniform": African American girls in an elite high school and the importance of habitus. *Anthropology & Education Quarterly, 30*(3), 317–342.

Hughes, S. A. (2008). Toward "good enough methods" for autoethnography in a graduate education course: Trying to resist the matrix with another promising red pill. *Educational Studies, 43*(2), 125–143.

Hughes, S. A., & Pennington, J. L. (2016). *Autoethnography: Process, product, and possibility for critical social research.* Thousand Oaks, CA: Sage Publications.

Hughes, S. A., Pennington, J. L., & Makris, S. (2012). Translating autoethnography across the AERA standards: Toward understanding autoethnographic scholarship as empirical research. *Educational Researcher, 41*(6), 209–219.

Hurston, Z. N. (1925, May). Color struck. *Opportunity Magazine.*

Hurston, Z. N. (1942). *Dust tracks on a road: An autobiography.* Chicago, IL: University of Illinois Press.

Ibrahim, A., & Steinberg, S. R. (Eds.). (2014). *Critical youth studies reader.* New York, NY: Peter Lang.

James, S. D. (2009, April 14). When words can kill: 'That's so gay'. *ABC News.* Retrieved from http://abcnews.go.com/Health/MindMoodNews/story?id=7328091

Jarmon, R. (2013). *Black girls are from the future: Essays on race, digital creativity and pop culture.* Washington, D.C.: Jarmon Media.

Jaschik, S. (2015, July 1). The professor who wasn't fired. *Inside Higher Ed.* Retrieved from https://www.insidehighered.com/news/2015/07/01/twitter-explodes-false-reports-u-memphis-fired-professor-why

Johnson, A. (2014). Confessions of a video vixen: My autocritography of sexuality, desire, and memory. *Text and Performance Quarterly, 34*(2), 182–200.

Johnson, E. P. (1998). Feeling the spirit in the dark: Expanding notions of the sacred in the African-American gay community. *Callaloo, 21*(2), 399–416.

Johnson, E. P. (2003a). The pot is brewing: Marlon Rigg's Black is...Black ain't. In E. P. Johnson & M. Henderson (Eds.), *Black queer studies: A critical anthology* (pp. 1–20). Durham, NC: Duke University Press.

Johnson, E. P. (2003b). Strange fruit: A performance about identity politics. *The Drama Review, 47*(2), 88–116.

Johnson, E. P. (2005). "Quare" studies, or (almost) everything I know about queer studies I learned from my grandmother. In E. P. Johnson & M. Henderson (Eds.), *Black queer studies: A critical anthology* (pp. 124–160). Durham, NC: Duke University Press.

Johnson, E. P. (2006). Black performance studies: Genealogies, politics, futures. In D. S. Madison & J. Hamera (Eds.), *The Sage handbook of performance studies* (pp. 446–463). Thousand Oaks, CA: Sage Publications.

Johnson, E. P., & Henderson, M. G. (2005). Introduction: Queering Black studies/"quaring" queer studies. In E. P. Johnson & M. Henderson (Eds.), *Black queer studies: A critical anthology* (pp. 1–20). Durham, NC: Duke University Press.

Johnson, L. L., Jackson, J., Stovall, D. O., & Baszile, D. T. (2017). Loving blackness to death: (Re)imagining ELA classrooms in a time of racial chaos. *English Journal, 106*(4), 60.

Johnson, W. (Interviewer), & Finney, N. (Interviewee). (2012). *Nikky Finney: Heart, truth, and justice* [Interview transcript]. Retrieved from http://www.lambdaliterary.org/features/01/23/nikky-finney-heart-power-and-justice/

Jones, D. (2007, December 12). Chicago gay community regards new gay murder with dismay. *Gay Black Male News.* Retrieved from http://www.gbmnews.com/articles/2194/1/Chicago-Gay-Community-Regards-New-Gay-Murder-With-Dismay/Page1.html

Jones, J. L. (1997). "Sista docta": Performance as critique of the academy. *The Drama Review, 21*(2), 51–67.

Jones, J. L. (2002). Performance ethnography: The role of embodiment in cultural authenticity. *Theatre Topics, 12*(1), 1–15.

Jones, J. L. (2005). Cast a wide net. *Theatre Journal, 57*(4), 598–600.

Jones, N. (2010). *Between good and ghetto: African American girls and inner-city violence.* New Brunswick, NJ: Rutgers University Press.

Jordan, J. (1969). *Who look at me.* New York, NY: Ty Crowell Co.

Jordan, J. (1985). Nobody mean more to me than you and the future life of Willie Jordan. In J. Jordan (Ed.), *On call: Political essays* (pp. 123–139). Cambridge, MA: South End Press.

Jordan, J. (2002). *But some of us did not die: New and selected essays of June Jordan.* New York, NY: Basic/Civitas Books.

Jordan, J. (2005). Poem about my rights. In *Directed by desire: The collected poems of June Jordan* (pp. 309–311). Port Townsend, WA: Copper Canyon Press.

Karimi, F., Berryman, K., & Ford, D. (2016, July 27). Who was Freddie Gray, whose death has reignited protests against police? *CNN News.* Retrieved from http://www.cnn.com/2015/05/01/us/freddie-gray-who-is-he/

Kasl, E., & Yorks, L. (2010). "Whose inquiry is this anyway?" Money, power, reports, and collaborative inquiry. *Adult Educational Quarterly, 60*, 315–338. doi:10.1177/0741713609347367

Keeler, J. (2014, April 29). On Cliven Bundy's 'ancestral rights'. *The Nation.* Retrieved from https://www.thenation.com/article/cliven-bundys-ancestral-rights/

King, J. (2014, August 8). One year later, justice remains illusive for Islan Nettles. *Colorlines.* Retrieved from http://colorlines.com/archives/2014/08/one_year_after_islan_nettles_murder_justice_remains_illusive.html

King, W. (2014). "Prematurely knowing of evil things": The sexual abuse of African American girls and young women in slavery and freedom. *Journal of African American History, 99*(3), 173–196.

Kinloch, V. (2006). *June Jordan: Her life and letters.* Westport, CT: Greenwood Publishing Group.

Kinnard, M. (2017, December 7). Ex-South Carolina cop who shot fleeing Walter Scott in the back sentenced to 20 years in prison. *Chicago Tribune.* Retrieved from http://www.chicagotribune.com/news/nationworld/ct-michael-slager-sentencing-20171207-story.html

Klevah. (2015, May). *Good lover* [Audio file]. Retrieved from https://soundcloud.com/klevah/klevah-golden-18-good-lover

LaBennett, O. (2011). *She's mad real: Popular culture and West Indian girls in Brooklyn.* New York, NY: NYU Press.

Ladner, J. A. (1971). *Tomorrow's tomorrow.* New York, NY: Doubleday & Company.

Langellier, K. (1999). Personal narrative, performance, performativity: Two or three things I know for sure. *Text and Performance Quarterly, 19*(2), 123–144.

Lapadat, J. C. (2018). Collaborative auto ethnography: An ethical approach to inquiry that makes sense. In N. K. Denzin & M. D. Giardina (Eds.), *Qualitative inquiry in the public sphere* (pp. 156–170). New York, NY: Routledge.

Lea, V., & Sims, E. J. (Eds.). (2008). *Undoing whiteness in the classroom: Critical educultural teaching approaches for social justice activism.* New York, NY: Peter Lang.

Leavy, P. (2010). *Method meets art: Arts-based research practice.* New York, NY: The Guilford Press.

Lei, J. L. (2003). (Un)necessary toughness? Those "loud Black girls" and those "quiet Asian boys." *Anthropology and Education Quarterly, 42*(2), 158–181.

Leland, J. (2013, May 29). Man killed in the village is remembered as outgoing and private. *The New York Times*. Retrieved from http://www.nytimes.com/2013/05/30/nyregion/mark-carson-gay-man-killed-in-greenwich-village-is-remembered.html?_r=0

Levenson, E., Park, M., & Simon, D. (2018, March 22). Sacramento police shot man holding cellphone in his grandmother's yard. *CNN News*. Retrieved from https://www.cnn.com/2018/03/22/us/sacramento-police-shooting/index.html/

Lightfoot, S. L. (1976). Socialization and education of young Black girls in school. *Teachers College Record, 78*(2), 239–262.

Lim, J. H. (2008). The road not taken: Two African-American girls' experiences with school mathematics. *Race Ethnicity and Education, 11*(3), 303–317.

Lionnet, F. (1993). Autoethnography: The an-archic style of dust tracks on a road. In H. L. Gates & K. A. Appiah (Eds.), *Zora Neale Hurston: Critical perspectives past and present* (pp. 241–266). New York, NY: Amistad.

Livingston, J., & Orion Home Video (Film). (1990). *Paris is burning*. New York, NY: Fox Lorber Home Video.

Lorde, A. (1982). *Zami: A new spelling of my name*. Berkeley, CA: Crossing Press.

Lorde, A. (1984). *Sister outsider*. Berkeley, CA: Crossing Press.

Lorde, A. (1990). *Need: A chorale for Black woman voices*. Latham, NY: Kitchen Table/Women of Color Press.

Lorde, A. (1995). *The Black unicorn*. New York, NY: W.W. Norton.

Lorde, A. (1997a). Outlines. In A. Lorde (Ed.), *The collected poems of Aude Lorde* (pp. 361–366). New York, NY: W. W. Norton.

Lorde, A. (1997b). *The cancer journals: Special edition*. San Francisco, CA: Aunt Lute.

Love, B. L. (2012). *Hip hop's li'l sistas speak: Negotiating hip hop identities and politics in the new south*. New York, NY: Peter Lang.

Love, B. L. (2014). "Too young for the marches but I remember these drums:" Recommended pedagogies for hip-hop based education and youth studies. In A. Ibrahim & S. R. Steinberg (Eds.), *Critical youth studies reader* (pp. 444–451). New York, NY: Peter Lang.

Lowery, W. (2016, August 2). Korryn Gaines, cradling child and shotgun, is fatally shot by police. *Washington Post*. Retrieved from https://www.washingtonpost.com/news/post-nation/wp/2016/08/02/korryn-gaines-is-the-ninth-black-woman-shot-and-killed-by-police-this-year/?utm_term=.0f7e80fb634d

Ludacris. (2015, March 31). *Good Lovin* [Recorded by Ludacris ft. Miguel]. New York, NY: Def Jam Recordings.

Madison, D. S. (2011). *Critical ethnography: Method, ethics, and performance*. Thousand Oaks, CA: Sage Publications.

Madison, D. S., & Hamera, J. (2006). Introduction: Performance studies at the intersections. In D. S. Madison & J. Hamera (Eds.), *The Sage handbook of performance studies* (pp. xi–xxv). Thousand Oaks, CA: Sage Publications.

Mahone, S. (Ed.). (1994). *Moon marked and touched by sun: Plays by African-American women*. New York, NY: Theatre Communications Group.

Majors, R., & Billson, J. M. (1993). *Cool pose: The dilemma of Black manhood in America*. New York, NY: Simon and Schuster.

McArthur, S. A., & Muhammad, G. E. (2017). Black muslim girls navigating multiple oppositional binaries through literacy and letter writing. *Educational Studies, 53*(1), 63–77.

McClaurin, I. (Ed.). (2001). *Black feminist anthropology: Theory, politics, praxis, and poetics*. New Brunswick, NJ: Rutgers University Press.

McClaurin, I. (2012). Black feminist auto/ethnography that makes you want to cry. *Insight News*. Retrieved from http://www.insightnews.com/2012/06/27/black-feminist-autoethnography-that-makes-you-want-to-cry/

McCorkel, J. A., & Myers, K. (2003). What difference does difference make: Position and privilege in the field. *Qualitative Sociology, 26*(2), 199–231.

McCready, L. T. (2004). Understanding the marginalization of gay and gender non-conforming Black male students. *Theory into Practice, 43*(2), 136–143.

McCready, L. T. (2010a). *Making space for diverse masculinities: Difference, intersectionality, and engagement in an urban high school*. New York, NY: Peter Lang.

McCready, L. T. (2010b). Black queer bodies, Afrocentric reform and masculine anxiety. *The International Journal of Critical Pedagogy, 3*(1), 52.

McCready, L. T. (2013). Conclusion to the special issue: Queer of color analysis: Interruptions and pedagogic possibilities. *Curriculum Inquiry, 43*(4), 512–522.

McKenzie, J. (2001). *Perform or else: From discipline to performance*. London: Routledge.

McKittrick, K. (2006). *Demonic grounds: Black women and the cartographies of struggle*. Minneapolis, MN: University of Minnesota Press.

McKittrick, K., & Woods, C. A. (Eds.). (2007). *Black geographies and the politics of place*. Cambridge, MA: South End Press.

Moreira, C., & Diversi, M. (2010). When janitors dare to become scholars. *International Review of Qualitative Research, 2*(4), 457–474.

Morris, E. W. (2007). "Ladies" or "loudies"? Perceptions and experiences of Black girls in classrooms. *Youth & Society, 38*(4), 490–515.

Morris, M. W. (2016). *Pushout: The criminalization of Black girls in schools*. New York, NY: The New Press.

Moten, F. (2003). *In the break: The aesthetics of the Black radical tradition*. Minneapolis, MN: University of Minnesota Press.

Mouse FX. (2015, November 25). *Underdog closing: A frog!* Retrieved from https://youtu.be/6dLxtIImtFU

Moynihan, D. P. (1965). *The Negro family: The case for national action*. Washington, DC: Office of Policy, Planning and Research. Retrieved from http://www.stanford.edu/~mrosenfe/Moynihan%27s%20The%20Negro%20Family.pdf

Muller, L., & The Poetry for the People Blueprint Collective. (1995). *June Jordan's poetry for the people: A revolutionary blueprint*. New York, NY: Routledge.

Nathan, R. (2005). *My freshman year: What a professor learned by becoming a student*. Ithaca, NY: Cornell University Press.

Nemiroff, R. (Ed.). (1969). *To be young, gifted, and Black: Lorraine Hansberry in her own words*. New York, NY: Vintage Books.

Norris, J. (2009). *Playbuilding as qualitative research: A participatory arts-based research*. Walnut Creek, CA: Left Coast Press.

Norris, J., Sawyer, R. D., & Lund, D. (2012). *Duoethnography: Dialogic methods for social, health, and educational research*. Walnut Creek, CA: Left Coast Press.

Orbe, M. P. (1998). *Constructing co-cultural theory: An explication of culture, power, and communication*. Thousand Oaks, CA: Sage Publications.

Pasque, P., Carducci, R., Kuntz, A., & Gildersleeve, R. (2012). *Qualitative inquiry for equity in higher education: Methodological innovations, implications, and interventions*. Hoboken, NJ: John Wiley & Sons.

Patton, S. (2014, November 26). In America, Black children don't get to be children. *The Washington Post*. Retrieved from https://www.washingtonpost.com/opinions/

in-america-black-children-dont-get-to-be-children/2014/11/26/a9e24756-74ee-11e4-a755-e32227229e7b_story.html?noredirect=on&utm_term=.102d78bfd537

Pennington, J. L. (2007). Silence in the classroom/whispers in the halls: Autoethnography as pedagogy in White pre-service teacher education. *Race Ethnicity and Education, 10*(1), 93–113.

Pensoneau-Conway, S. L., Adams, T. E., & Bolen, D. M. (2017). *Doing autoethnography.* Boston, MA: Sense Publishers.

Perry, T. (Ed.). (1996). *Teaching Malcolm X.* New York, NY: Routledge.

Phelan, P. (1992). *Unmarked: The politics of performance.* New York, NY: Routledge.

Philip, M. N. (2008). *Zong!* Middletown, CT: Wesleyan University Press.

Pollock, D. (2006). Performance trouble. In D. S. Madison & J. Hamera (Eds.), *The Sage handbook of performance studies* (pp. 1–8). Thousand Oaks, CA: Sage Publications.

Prier, D. D. (2012). *Culturally relevant teaching: Hip-hop pedagogy in urban schools.* New York, NY: Peter Lang.

Pritchard, E. D. (2013). For colored kids who committed suicide, our outrage isn't enough: Queer youth of color, bullying, and the discursive limits of identity and safety. *Harvard Educational Review, 83*(2), 320–345.

Pritchard, E. D. (2016). *Fashioning lives: Black queers and the politics of literacy.* Carbondale, IL: SIU Press.

Rappleye, H. (2014, August 25). Handcuffed Black youth shot himself to death, says coroner. *NBC News.* Retrieved from https://www.nbcnews.com/news/investigations/handcuffed-black-youth-shot-himself-death-says-coroner-n185016

Rector, K., & Gorelick, R. (2015, May 11). The Hippo, longtime anchor of Baltimore's gay community, to close this fall. *Baltimore Sun.* Retrieved from http://www.baltimoresun.com/features/gay-in-maryland/gay-matters/bs-bz-hippo-closing-20150511-story.html

Reed-Danahay, D. (1997). *Auto/ethnography: Rewriting the self and the social.* Oxford: Berg.

Richardson, E. B. (2013). *PHD to Ph.D.: How education saved my life.* New York, NY: New City Community Press.

Richardson, L. (1997). *Fields of play: Constructing an academic life.* New Brunswick, NJ: Rutgers University Press.

Richardson, L. (2000). Writing: A method of inquiry. In N. K. Denzin & Y. S. Lincoln (Eds.), *Handbook of qualitative research* (2nd ed., pp. 923–948). Thousand Oaks, CA: Sage Publications.

Richardson, L. (2002). Poetic representation of interviews. In J. F. Gubrium & J. A. Holstein (Eds.), *Handbook of interview research: Context and method* (pp. 822–891). Thousand Oaks, CA: Sage Publications.

Richardson, L., & St. Pierre, E. A. (2008). Writing: A method of inquiry. In N. K. Denzin & Y. S. Lincoln (Eds.), *Collecting and interpreting qualitative materials* (pp. 473–500). Thousand Oaks, CA: Sage Publications.

Rollock, N. (2007). Why Black girls don't matter: Exploring how race and gender shape academic success in an inner city school. *Support for Learning, 22*(4), 197–202.

Romo, J. J. (2005). Border pedagogy from the inside out: An autoethnographic study. *Journal of Latinos and Education, 4*(3), 193–210.

Rosaldo, R. (1989). *Culture and truth: The remaking of social analysis.* Boston, MA: Beacon Press.

Rose, J. (2018, April 5). Black man fatally shot in NYC after police mistake metal pipe for gun. *National Public Radio.* Retrieved from https://www.npr.org/2018/04/05/599895198/black-man-fatally-shot-in-nyc-after-police-mistake-metal-pipe-for-gun

Rose, M. (1990). *Lives on the boundary: A moving account of the struggles and achievements of America's educational underprepared.* New York, NY: Penguin.

Russel, C. (1999). *Experimental ethnography.* Durham, NC: Duke University Press.

Saldaña, J. (2003). Dramatizing data: A primer. *Qualitative Inquiry, 9*(2), 218–236.

Saldaña, J. (Ed.). (2005). *Ethnodrama: An anthology of reality theatre.* Lanham, MD: AltaMira Press.

Saldaña, J. (2006). This is not a performance text. *Qualitative Inquiry, 12*(6), 1091–1098. doi:10.1177/1077800406293239

Saldaña, J. (2008). Second chair: An autoethnodrama. *Research Studies in Music Education, 30*(2), 177–191.

Saldaña, J. (2011). *Fundamentals of qualitative research: Understanding qualitative research.* New York, NY: Oxford University Press.

Salinger, T. (2016, September 21). Fatal shooting of Korryn Gaines by Maryland police officer 'justified,' prosecutors say. *Daily News.* Retrieved from http://www.nydailynews.com/news/crime/fatal-shooting-korryn-gaines-justified-prosecutors-article-1.2801015

Sammus. (2016, March 25). *Mighty morphing* [Video file]. Retrieved from https://binged.it/2Ix4Z6Q

Sanchez, R. (2015, July 22). What we know about the controversy in Sandra Bland's death. *CNN News.* Retrieved from https://www.cnn.com/2015/07/21/us/texas-sandra-bland-jail-death-explain/index.html

Schechnner, R. (1985). *Between theatre and anthropology.* Philadelphia, PA: University of Pennsylvania Press.

Schmadeke, S., St. Clair, S., & Gorner, J. (2013, November 26). Prosecutors: Detective was 'reckless' in fatal off-duty shooting. *Chicago Tribune.* Retrieved from http://articles.chicagotribune.com/2013-11-26/news/chi-detective-charged-with-involuntary-manslaughter-in-fatal-shooting-20131125_1_involuntary-manslaughter-police-officer-detective-dante-servin

Sears, S. D. (2010). *Imagining Black womanhood: The negotiation of power and identity within the girls empowerment project.* Albany, NY: State University of New York Press.

Semuels, A. (2014, September 3). Detroit-area man gets 17 to 32 years for shooting visitor on porch. *Los Angeles Times.* Retrieved from http://www.latimes.com/nation/nationnow/la-na-nn-porch-killer-sentenced-20140903-story.html

Shakur, A. (2001). *Assata: An autobiography.* Chicago, IL: Lawrence Hill Books.

Shange, N. (1977). *For colored girls who have considered suicide/when the rainbow is enuf.* New York, NY: Macmillan Publishing.

Shapiro, E. (2015, December 28). One of these is the toy gun Tamir Rice was holding: prosecutors. *ABC News.* Retrieved from https://abcnews.go.com/US/toy-gun-tamir-rice-holding-prosecutors/story?id=35982086

Shapiro, L. (2014, August 27). 'These murders are a steady drumbeat': A year after trans NYC murder, community on edge. *Huffington Post.* Retrieved from http://www.huffingtonpost.com/2014/08/27/islan-nettles_n_5721874.html

Shapiro, T. R. (2017, June 27). Study: Black girls viewed as 'less innocent' than White girls. *The Washington Post.* Retrieved from https://www.washingtonpost.com/local/education/study-black-girls-viewed-as-less-innocent-than-white-girls/2017/06/27/3fbedc32-5ae1-11e7-a9f6-7c3296387341_story.html?utm_term=.be7f101c0631

Shujaa, M. J. (1998). *Too much schooling, too little education: A paradox of Black life in White societies.* Trenton, NJ: Africa World Press.

Simon, D. (Producer). (2008). *The wire* [Television series]. New York, NY: Home Box Office.

Simon, M. (2009, April 23). My bullied son's last day on earth. *CNN News*. Retrieved from http://www.cnn.com/2009/US/04/23/bullying.suicide/index.html

Smith, E. J., & Harper, S. R. (2015). *Disproportionate impact of K-12 school suspension and expulsion on Black students in southern states* (Center for the Study of Race and Equity in Education). Philadelphia, PA: University of Pennsylvania. Retrieved from https://equity.gse.upenn.edu/sites/default/files/publications/Smith_Harper_Report.pdf

SOLHOT. *Saving our lives hear our truths*. Retrieved March 16, 2018, from http://solhot.weebly.com

Somerville, S. B. (2000). *Queering the color line: Race and the invention of homosexuality in American culture*. Durham, NC: Duke University Press.

Spillers, H. J. (1987). Mama's baby, papa's maybe: An American grammar book. *Diacritics, 17*(2), 65–81.

Spry, T. (2001). Performing autoethnography: An embodied methodological praxis. *Qualitative Inquiry, 7*(6), 706–732.

Spry, T. (2011). *Body, paper, stage: Writing and performing autoethnography*. Walnut Creek, CA: Left Coast Press.

Spry, T. (2016). *Autoethnography and the other: Unsettling power through Utopian performatives*. New York, NY: Routledge.

Stevens, J. W. (2002). *Smart and sassy: The strengths of inner-city Black girls*. New York, NY: Oxford University Press.

Stitzlein, S. M. (2008). *Breaking bad habits of race and gender: Transforming identity in schools*. Boulder, CO: Rowman & Littlefield Publishers.

Stutzman, R. (2015, February 25). *Middle school suicide: Boy found dead on campus had not talked about killing himself*. Retrieved from http://www.orlandosentinel.com/features/education/os-gun-suicide-school-campus-seminole-20150225-story.html

Talbert, S., & Lesko, N. (2014). Historicizing youth studies. In A. Ibrahim & S. R Steinberg (Eds.), *Critical youth studies reader* (pp. 26–37). New York, NY: Peter Lang.

Tinsley, O. E. N. (2008). Black atlantic, queer atlantic: Queer imaginings of the middle passage. *GLQ: A Journal of Lesbian and Gay Studies, 14*(2–3), 191–215.

Tuck, E., & Yang, K. W. (2014). Unbecoming claims: Pedagogies of refusal in qualitative research. *Qualitative Research, 20*(6), 811–818.

Walker, A. (1983). *In search of our mothers' gardens: Womanist prose*. San Diego, CA: Harcourt, Brace, Jovanich.

Warren, C. A. (2014). Perspective divergence and the mis-education of Black boys…like me. *Perspective, 5*(2), 134–149.

Watkins, W. H., Lewis, J. H., Chou, V. (Eds.). (2001). *Race and education: The roles of history and society in educating African American students*. Boston, MA: Allyn & Bacon.

Weems, M. E. (2003). *Public education and the imagination-intellect: I speak from the wound in my mouth*. New York, NY: Peter Lang.

Weems, M. E., Callier, D. M., & Boylorn, R. M. (2014). Love, peace and soooooul: The fire this time writers' group. *Cultural Studies ↔ Critical Methodologies, 14*(4), 333–337.

We Levitate. (2016, February). *Take care* [Audio file]. Retrieved from https://welevitate.bandcamp.com/album/how-i-feel-ep

Williams, T. (2011, September 26). *Jailed for switching her daughters' school district*. Retrieved from https://www.nytimes.com/2011/09/27/us/jailed-for-switching-her-daughters-school-district.html

REFERENCES

Winn, M. T. (2011). *Girl time: Literacy, justice, and the school-to-prison pipeline*. New York, NY: Teachers College Press.

Wyatt, J., Gale, K., Russell, L., Pelias, R. J., & Spry, T. (2011). How writing touches. *International Review of Qualitative Research, 4*(3), 253–277.

Wynter, S., & McKittrick, K. (2015). *Sylvia Wynter: On being human as praxis*. Durham, NC: Duke University Press.

Young, H. B. (2005). *Haunting capital: Memory, text and the Black diasporic body*. Lebanon, NH: Dartmouth College Press.

Young, H. B. (2010). *Embodying Black experience: Stillness, critical memory, and the Black body*. Ann Arbor, MI: The University of Michigan Press.

Zebra Katz. (2012, January 18). *Ima read* (ft. Njena Reddd Foxxx) [Video File]. Retrieved from https://www.youtube.com/watch?v=oo4Sqt2Bmag

Zita, J. N. (1998). *Body talk: Philosophical reflections on sex and gender*. New York, NY: Columbia University Press.

ABOUT THE AUTHORS

Durell M. Callier, PhD, is an assistant professor in the Department of Educational Leadership at Miami University. His research and teaching focuses on the ways that Black and queer performances of culture and memory through literary texts, embodied performances, and visual art create alternative archives for understanding Black lives and act as educative sites for staging critical resistance and practicing and actualizing freedom. Primarily, his areas of research include Black Performance, Critical Qualitative Methods, Black Feminist and Queer Theory, and Cultural Theory. An artist-scholar, Callier is the co-visionary of an arts-based collective, Hill L. Waters (www.hilllwaters.com), which enacts Black, queer world-making as an embodied pedagogy, research site, and publicly engaged practice.

Dominique C. Hill, PhD, is a citizen of the world, committed to illuminating the knowledge and cultural production of Black life. Hill uses auto/ethnography, feminist theory, and performance studies refined in Black feminist embodied and creative methodologies to curate and reimagine Black girls' and women's educational experiences. Her current research examines Black girlhood and Black girls' embodied pedagogies and experiences of carcerality in and beyond schools. Hill is the co-visionary of an arts-based collective, Hill L. Waters (www.hilllwaters.com), which enacts Black, queer world-making as an embodied pedagogy, research site, and publicly engaged practice. She is the 2017 recipient of the Illinois Distinguished Qualitative Dissertation Award in experimental design, and is a visiting assistant professor of Black Studies at Amherst College.

INDEX

Made in the USA
Middletown, DE
05 February 2020

84238121R10088